Fight For Your Best Life:

The Step-By-Step Self-defense Guide to Personal Empowerment, Protecting Your Loved Ones, and Living Fearless

John Timothy Brewer Jr.

For more information, email info@mindshieldandspear.com.

ISBN. 979-8-88759-943-4 paperback

ISBN: 979-8-88759-944-1 - ebook

Library of Congress Control Number: 2023915916

To my Dad, for you taught me understanding.

To my Mom, for you taught me determination.

To my Grandeddy, for you taught me vision.

To my Granny, for you taught me grit.

To my Grandma, for you taught me benevolence.

To my sisters, for you taught me perspective.

To my children, for you show me what is truly important.

To my wife, for you are my partner, my companion, and my better half.

Want Personalized Guidance?

Scan the QR code below to schedule a free consultation with a consultant at Mind, Shield, and Spear Consulting Group. Using the principles presented in this book, we will assist you in creating a safe and enjoyable life for you and your loved ones.

You can also visit www.mindshieldandspear.com for links to additional information and services.

Table of Contents

Introduction

"Self-defense is not only our right; it is our duty."

Ronald Reagan

We live in a world where danger is widespread and diverse. If you are reading this book, odds are you have had moments where you have felt unsafe, worried about the safety of your loved ones, or have seen or heard about unnerving events in the news. The unfortunate truth is that humans are a constant and continuous threat to other humans. Equally, humans are capable of compassion, selfless achievement, and pursuing a noble purpose. That is quite a range. There are many beliefs and theories based on biology, spirituality, religion, and quantum cosmology as to why this spectrum is the condition of our existence. This book does not act to study any one of these beliefs or theories; instead, it only acknowledges the state of the world and acts to enable those who mean well against those who intend violence.

1

This book is meant to provide a foundational framework and tools for individuals of all backgrounds to be more confident, empowered, and—most importantly—safe from harm. It is designed to enable and empower any individual who wishes to prevent victimization of themselves and those they care about.

Although a majority of the concepts taught in this book will ultimately be applied to self-defense scenarios, they can also be applied to any situation where there is a risk to personal safety. These events may be initiated by individuals with malicious intent, acts of nature, or events that are accidental in nature such as motor vehicle collisions, lapses in judgment, or instances of Murphy's Law—the idea that everything that can go wrong will go wrong.

As with all things, skill is built through experience. However, considering self-defense pertains to life-or-death scenarios, it is difficult for those outside of the military and law enforcement to gain the experience needed to be fully comfortable with the concepts and practice of self-protection. That's where this book comes in. The concepts introduced in this book can be applied to crossing the street, home invasions, and everything in between. Ultimately, the goal is to enable you as a capable, responsible person to be able to effectively protect yourself and your loved ones. My hope is that the content of this book will alleviate your anxiety and free up your time and effort so they can be spent doing what is important to you.

I have seen, firsthand, the importance of empowerment. Working directly with individuals in war-torn countries as a member of US Army Special Forces, I know certain problems can only be solved by the people who are directly affected. When third parties act to take the responsibilities away from others, problems become unnecessarily more complicated. Additionally, through the steadfast culture of Green Berets, I have learned the art of problem-solving through determination, ingenuity, and most of all, common sense. Yes, war is much different than personal self-defense events, but the fine details and individual tactics within warfare are parallel to all dangerous encounters.

This book is not meant to tell you what to do, how to think, or how to act. It will not provide techniques on how to disarm armed assailants, put people asleep with an ancient mystical pinkie hold, or try to turn you into John Wick, John Rambo, or another John Brewer (one is already too much). The concepts in this book are far too dynamic to dive that deeply into—not to mention, many of the skills that can be utilized in self-defense are better explained and performed by in-person instruction. Rather, this book will guide you through concepts and practices from a variety of disciplines that are designed to assist you in finding solutions that align with your Life Goals and overall lifestyle.

Most concepts that are introduced stay at a high-level overview to provide a template for universal use. If you are interested in learning more about any particular aspect of this book, please visit my website, www. mindshieldandspear.com, for additional information and an updated list of supplementary resources.

This book is composed of five sections. Each section builds on the next by elaborating or adding new concepts to those already addressed. You might be tempted to skip directly to the section specifically about actions during self-defense scenarios, but I implore you to read the book in its entirety, as it is designed to provide a complete solution to better empower you as a person of value and purpose.

Section One, Internal Awareness and Personal Development, will introduce concepts for self-development and provide the tools needed to understand where you might be in your life and how to get where you want to go. This section will skim the surface of the fields of psychology, personal development, and optimal performance. Section Two, External Factors, introduces and analyzes external factors relevant to safety and self-protection. The main goal in this section is to develop an analytical process that you can adopt to assist you in identifying and evaluating the world outside of your usual perception. Section Three, Prevention and Preparedness, is where we begin to formulate constructive and practical solutions. We will develop prevention strategies that act to prevent, mitigate, and lessen risk of harm. This section takes everything you worked on in Sections One and Two and incorporates them into a comprehensive plan tailored to your capabilities and needs. Section Four, The Safety Event, reviews concepts and principles that relate and apply to life threatening events. The aim is to provide general principles to consider and follow, which then can be applied to any scenario. Lastly, Section Five, The Aftermath, aims to prepare you for the possible impact and repercussions of a Safety Event. This section introduces and reviews concepts of trauma recovery and rehabilitative processes.

To best utilize this book, I recommend:

1. Do a complete read-through before conducting each chapter's Call to Action, which are activities for you to complete found at the end of the chapter.

2. Once you have completed one read-through, review each chapter summary and complete it's Call to Action. Don't try and complete all Call to Actions in one sitting. This should be seen as a daily practice, whether you work on it in the morning before starting your day, during lunch, before bed, or anytime in between. I recommend setting aside ten to thirty minutes per day to work on the Call to Actions to maintain consistency and to avoid burnout. Also, don't worry

about making it perfect, as each product can be treated as a living document and modified as many times as needed.

3. Visit my website, www.mindshieldandspear. com, where you can find the Call to Action (CTA) Workbook as well as other resources.

4. Refer to the Complementary Readings found at the end of the book for my top recommendations for supplementary readings.

5. Take what you need and leave what you don't. Most importantly, make it your own.

Overall, this book is meant to be a comprehensive guide to support you through life's toughest challenges, since it is my belief that if you can handle a life-or-death crisis, you can handle anything. The effects of this book will extend far greater than just individual safety, as this book could help foster a safer and less dangerous world. High hopes indeed, but still something worth fighting for. Literally.

But before we begin, we have to discuss a tool that is universally used but rarely mastered: the problem-solving cycle.

The Problem-Solving Cycle

"As the world we live in is so unpredictable, the ability to learn and to adapt to change is imperative, alongside creativity, problem-solving, and communication skills."

Alain Dehaze

The problem-solving cycle is as simple as it sounds: a reliable and flexible methodology for identifying problems and finding solutions. We use it every day to confront minor and major problems in our lives, everything from a sudden flat tire to figuring out what to eat for dinner (which, we can all agree, is a *major* problem). A common theme throughout this book is incorporating the problem-solving cycle and analytic processes to prevent and resolve self-defense scenarios safely. At its essence, self-defense is just problem-solving in high-stress, high-stakes scenarios. Although specifically applied to scenarios in this book, the skill of problem-solving will translate to, and benefit you, in all aspects of your life—and yes, it is most definitely a skill. The key is to establish a standard problem-solving system that will initially be used consciously and deliberately until, with enough practice, it becomes the way your mind automatically processes information.

As you will see, problem-solving is a continuous cycle rather than a process with a definitive ending. The cycle starts by identifying the problem. This will usually be blatantly obvious, as it likely is a problem that is disrupting your normal routine. It can also be vague in the sense you will need to analyze a situation to find out what the problem actually is (i.e., general stress and anxiety). Due to the seriousness of the problem, our example will be based on figuring out what to eat for dinner.

The second step is analyzing the factors related to the problem. There are many analytical methods, but in general, the process is to gather all relevant information, evaluate the information for its key elements, and formulate raw data into usable, coherent information. When analyzing solutions for dinner, we consider the time and resources it will take to cook, restaurants in the area that have a takeout option, whether we have enough money for a sit-down restaurant, and of course, if all parties can agree on the type of cuisine.

The third step in the problem-solving cycle is to develop courses of action or possible solutions. This is a whole process within itself, as there is a lot of strategy involved in developing solutions. This is usually the point in the dinner conversation when someone sharply says, "Look, would you rather heat up a frozen pizza or just order delivery?"

Once such a direct question is asked, others are forced to consider the proposed courses of action. Does the frozen pizza have the toppings I want? Can I wait forty-five minutes for pizza delivery before I get hangry? This is the fourth step: weighing the courses of action and developing contingencies. Done in real time, the fourth step is sometimes omitted, since once a solution is established, it is acted on. However, when planning ahead, all possible solutions should be weighed against considered factors to ensure completeness and effectiveness.

The fifth step is to implement the chosen course of action, AKA the solution. Finally, the decision has been made to order pizza from everyone's favorite pizzeria. Fifty minutes later, the pizza arrives, and—wouldn't you know it—they put onions on the plain cheese pizza.

Adapting to the circumstances, you decide to pick the onions off, and after all that trouble, you finally get to eat the dinner you worked so hard to acquire. This adjustment was the sixth and final step. You must monitor the situation and *adapt* as needed. Adaptations could require the full implementation of the problem-solving cycle or just an abbreviated version that pinpoints specific details.

Below you will find a graphical representation of the problem-solving cycle. This depiction drives home the cyclic nature of problem-solving and its continuous process.

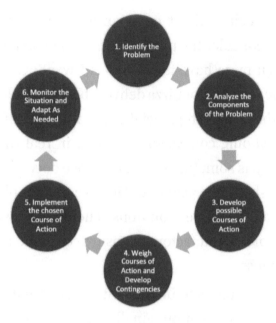

Figure 1: Problem-Solving Cycle

As you can see, the problem-solving cycle is pretty straightforward, but takes time to master, as there are an infinite number of solutions to an infinite number of problems. The good news is you do not have to solve every problem in the world. Just the ones that pertain to you and what is important to you. And this is where we will begin in the next section.

Section One:
Internal Awareness and Personal Development

"There are three things extremely hard: steel, a diamond, and to know one's self."

Benjamin Franklin

What is it that you are fighting to protect? Why is it you want to protect yourself and others? Of course, you could answer that you just don't like physical or emotional pain and do not want your loved ones to ever be victimized. Although true, the complete answer is much deeper than that.

Just living through life is not enough—we must live our best life. Now, I can't tell you what your "best life" looks like, as it is different for everyone. It should be exclusive to you and serve as your motivation for completing this book and taking responsibility for your safety and for those you care about. However, I can give you a hint on what is the basis for figuring out your "best life" - the key is understanding yourself. (Okay, that's not so much a hint as it is the answer) Once we understand our needs, wants, and goals, we can focus our efforts on fulfilling them and, equally as important, ensuring they are secure and protected. Although the subject matter of this section does have philosophical undertones, it produces real-world, practical outcomes that are needed in order to establish real security in one's life. Once security is established and practiced, you can apply these same concepts introduced in this section to all aspects of your life. Section One is all about getting personal—personal awareness, personal development, and personal empowerment.

Chapter 1:
Maslow's Hierarchy of Needs

"What a man can be, he must be. This need we call self-actualization."

Abraham Maslow

In 1943, an American psychologist named Abraham Maslow introduced the Hierarchy of Needs as a means to depict human motivation. The theory has gained widespread popularity and is used to this day. Maslow's Hierarchy of Needs is even the quasi-spiritual inspiration for writing this book. Conceptually, it serves as the broader reason why personal security and safety are not only vital for a healthy, sustainable life— but also for a purposeful life. This is not to say the theory should be treated as gospel, as it is just theory. There are some psychologists and researchers who feel the theory has not been, and cannot be, empirically tested. Others say the theory is too narrow. This is the way of science—everything that can be questioned should be questioned. My proposition is that the theory, and every level of the hierarchy, provides transferable skills that can be used to enable you to transcend the hierarchy, and this is how Maslow's Hierarchy of Needs provides practical value.

The theory explains that humans have needs on three fundamental levels: basic needs, psychological needs, and self-fulfillment needs, each building on one another. (Note: The theory has been modified with the addition of cognitive, aesthetic, and self-transcendence needs, but we are only concerned with the classical depiction, as it provides a more focused scope.) The theory is most commonly understood through the model of a pyramid, shown in Figure 2. The pyramid model places the foundational needs at the base of the pyramid that lead to the peak of the pyramid which demonstrates the pinnacle of one's life.

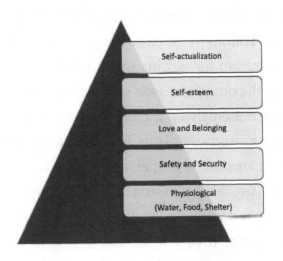

Figure 2: Pyramid Model of Maslow's Hierarchy of Needs

The pyramid's bottom two levels cover the basic needs to sustain life, such as food, shelter, water, safety, and protection. The middle two levels cover psychological needs, which encompasses belongingness, love, and self-esteem, usually fostered by our friends, family, and loved ones. The peak of the pyramid is considered to be the level of self-actualization, or the fulfillment of one's potential in life, such as reaching Life Goals or accomplishing bucket list items.

Maslow originally theorized that in order to reach self-actualization, one must meet all the needs below it. However, he later clarified that the fulfillment of each level does not need to be one hundred percent complete to be able to ascend up the pyramid. Rather, needs can be fulfilled concurrently or partially, as the nature of life is fluctuant instead of strictly linear. Look at marriage as an example; some marry early in life, while others tie the knot a little bit later. Heck, some like it so much they do it multiple times. Either way, the hierarchy shows that no matter our stage in life, we are constantly working to fulfill one need or the other. No matter if all the needs must be met or only portions of each—it is my belief that the hierarchy provides general direction and a natural progression of growth and development.

One way I like to explain Maslow's Hierarchy of Needs is through the metaphor of the hierarchy forming a house. In addition to adding more relatable imagery, the house metaphor depicts how the hierarchy is a fluid relationship of cause and effect. As with us, a house goes through changes, repairs, and maintenance and is made up of critical elements that all combine to form one comprehensive, functional unit. For a house to exist, it must have a foundation, walls, doors, windows, and a roof.

Physiological needs serve as the foundation. A house, even if completely built, will not stand for long without a solid foundation. The next layer, and the focus of this book, is safety needs. safety needs make up the walls, doors, windows, and roof—everything that keeps the inside contents safe from the elements outside of the house. Next, we have psychological needs of love, belonging, and self-esteem. These are all the loved ones inside the house, everything from pets to plants to people, who care for us and vice versa. And lastly, there is self-actualization. Instead of a physical representation, this is the point where the house becomes a home. Once all the elements are present and foster the perfectly tailored environment, the house is no longer just a structure, for now it fulfills a higher sense of purpose.

That sense of purpose is the ultimate goal of this book. Maslow's Hierarchy of Needs will provide the framework we'll use for life management skills and, more specifically, the natural progression of transferable skills, which are constantly and continuously developed and built upon through each level of the pyramid.

The problem-solving cycle can be used here as well, as each need can be viewed as a problem needing to be solved. The pursuit of fulfilling physiological needs teaches the skills for problem-solving, sustainment, resourcefulness, procurement, and so on. After that, the problem moves up the pyramid. The pursuit of fulfilling safety needs builds upon the skills gained from the physiological level and adds social skills, physical ability, awareness, self-confidence, and so on. Those same skills can then be used to fulfill psychological needs, which act to establish and build bonds with others. Until eventually, you reach a point in your life where all your values, experiences, and abilities lead you to not only finding your purpose in life, but with all the tools needed to achieve it.

This is why we will focus on security and safety. They are needs that must be met for a happy, fulfilled, and sustainable life, but as I said in the introduction, they may be difficult to completely satisfy without proper development and consideration. By applying the principles taught in this book, you will be able to adequately satisfy your safety and protection needs while also acquiring transferable skills that will assist you in all aspects of your life. Together, we'll build our house from the foundation up so that it can weather any storm.

Chapter 1 Review

Points of Emphasis:

❖ Maslow's Hierarchy of Needs is a theory, often depicted as a pyramid, designed to explain the link between basic human needs, psychological needs, and self-fulfillment needs to reach self-actualization.

❖ Needs do not need to be met in order. However, basic needs to sustain life and safety needs should be fulfilled as soon as possible to ensure health and safety.

❖ Safety needs include protection from physical and emotional harm.

Perspective:

❖ Maslow's Hierarchy of Needs is a conceptual framework that can mean different things for different people. Similar to how a fortune cookie provides a vague fortune that allows it to be interpreted by the receiver. Like many things in life, there is not a one-size-fits-all solution. Additionally, not all solutions can be, or should be, handed to us by others. Our most optimal solution is created by ourselves.

Call to Action:

☐ Complete the Maslow's Hierarchy of Needs Worksheet in the CTA Workbook.

Chapter 2:
Aligning Core Values and Purpose

"What is necessary to change a person is to change his awareness of himself."

Abraham Maslow

Now that we have reviewed the purpose and foundational "why" of this book, it's time to explore our individual purpose and foundational "why." Alignment is a key element of harmony in every aspect of life, especially self-alignment. There is no such thing as a healthy relationship, a job you enjoy, meaningful friendships, fulfilling hobbies or entertainment, unless your Core Values and personality traits align with them.

Here, we will ensure your Safety Goals align with your Core Values. Doing so will create a seamless, self-guided transition from inspiration, to motivation, to action. A self-assessment serves as the focal point from which everything else will originate. As with any problem set, we must first identify the elements that are present and significant before we can make a plan to add, remove, or make changes. This assessment is an important step, both for this chapter and beyond—the information that we find from a self-assessment will later be used to ensure we are aligning our goals with our values, interests, and overall lifestyle.

There is a three-step process in the self-assessment. The first step is identifying Core Values, the second step is to create Safety Goals that support your Core Values, and the last step is to create Life Goals that align with your true life's ambitions once your safety needs are met. In taking it a step further, by formulating Life Goals, we are creating another point of alignment. All these points give us a better sense of who we are and what we need. It is possible to create and implement effective Safety Goals without Life Goals. However, without the clear connection, it is possible that we may omit a certain aspect of security coverage that is needed for complete safety and protection. This entire process aims to identify who we are, analyze our values, and develop goals and courses of action that will satisfy our safety and self-defense needs.

My Core Values lie with my family and caring for them. I assume the same also applies to many of you reading this book. My family is my motivation to continuously develop skills—safety skills or otherwise—that enable me to better care for them. They are my constant reminder to study or train when I'm having an off day or feeling sorry for myself. They are the entire reason why I am writing this book, as I would like to share the methods I use to help others care for their families as well. My Safety Goals all revolve around keeping my family away from harm and guaranteeing a strategic advantage if an event was to arise. My Life Goal is to assist and guide others as they look to meet their safety needs so they can focus on living a fruitful and blissful life rather than merely surviving.

Self-Assessment

Identifying Core Values

The first step in this self-assessment is to identify your Core Values. Core Values are principles or beliefs that a person views as being of central importance. You might be saying, "Well, of course I know myself. How could I not? I am me." Believe it or not, there are times when our own perspective of ourselves is not the complete picture—or even a fully accurate picture. To make sure you have the ideal perspective of your true self, all you need to do is take around ten minutes to think about what values are important to you and what goals you have.

You can answer these questions to help guide you:

Positive	Negative	Neutral
1. What brings you joy?	1. What causes you pain?	1. What advice would you give to your younger self?
2. Who are the people you look up to? How would you describe them?	2. Who are the people you avoid? How would you describe them?	2. How do you envision your life when you are older?
3. What are the memories you cherish? What were you doing?	3. What are the memories you rebuke? What were you doing?	

With the answers to these questions, look for commonalities and trends. This will lead you to the Core Values you find to be more important and relevant to you. From my experience answering the same questions, I noticed the topic of my family continued surfacing in my explanations for each. What brings me joy? My family and more specifically watching my daughter grow and develop. What memories do I cherish? Holidays and special occasions where the entire family makes an appearance. How do I envision my life when I am older? Contently rocking in my favorite rocking chair on the back porch as I watch my children and dogs play a rambunctious game of hide-n-seek.

Answers to the positive set of questions will lead you directly to Core Values by showing you what brings you happiness in life, while answers from the negative set of questions will show you the opposite of what you value. Ideally, the opposite of your answer to the negative questions will be an easily definable Core Value. If not, you might need the help of a thesaurus to narrow down a definable trait. Answers to the neutral set of questions should also ideally lead you to Core Values, but they are also designed to help you begin to formulate what your goals will be in the last step of our self-assessment.

Some values will be clearly stated within the answers, such as answers regarding who you look up to and who you avoid. It's likely you wrote down a value as the reason why. I look up to different members of my family, as they each embody aspiring qualities for me to emulate. My father was easygoing, my mother is tenacious, my grandfather was goal-oriented, and my grandmothers were independent. Altogether, they provide a template for the best version of myself to become.

For other answers, you might need to evaluate what Core Value is the basis for your answer or best fits. For example, if a negative memory we try not to think about is the time we were embarrassed in high school during a public speech, then we could infer at the time there might have been a lack of self-confidence, courage, or gumption which caused the embarrassment. By focusing on traits that would have improved the situation, we may find desired Core Values. These values will serve as the foundation for your goals, habits, and lifestyle.

To help you identify Core Values, try using the list below as a reference. Scan the words to see if any of them speak to you. If they do, ask yourself why, and you may find an alignment where you didn't expect one.

Acceptance	Contribution	Happiness
Authenticity	Courage	Honesty
Achievement	Creativity	Humor
Adventure	Curiosity	Independence
Authority	Education	Influence
Autonomy	Efficiency	Inner Harmony
Balance	Enjoyment	Inspiration
Beauty	Enthusiasm	Justice
Boldness	Expertise	Kindness
Compassion	Determination	Knowledge
Challenge	Fairness	Leadership
Citizenship	Faith	Learning
Commitment	Fame	Love
Community	Friendships	Loyalty
Competency	Fun	Meaningful Work
Consistency	Growth	Motivation

Openness	Relationships	Spirituality
Optimism	Reliability	Stability
Peace	Religion	Success
Performance	Reputation	Status
Pleasure	Respect	Tradition
Poise	Responsibility	Trustworthiness
Popularity	Security	Wealth
Positivity	Self-control	Wisdom
Pragmatism	Self-respect	Vitality
Recognition	Service	Youthfulness

Take your time, and you'll soon find your Core Values. Ideally, we should have around five, but don't worry about recognizing them immediately. Once you've found the ones that resonate, you'll know your Core Values in the same way you know what you want for dinner when someone says it out loud.

Safety Goals

Once you identify your Core Values, the second step in our self-assessment is to create Safety Goals. Your Core Values should provide the who or what you want to protect, maybe the when or the where security consideration is needed, and definitely how you want to go about doing it. In addition to using your Core Values, your life experiences, and those of others, will assist you in narrowing down what your Safety Goals should focus on.

All goals, safety or otherwise, should follow the SMART goal principle. SMART is an acronym that stands for specific, measurable, attainable, relevant, and timely. Just like the problem-solving cycle, this acronym is a tool to help us navigate our goals, while also proving useful in all other facets of life. Let's break SMART down, letter by letter.

"Specific" dictates the goal must contain precise details. For example, if your goal is to ensure your family is safe from harm, the goal should focus on identifying a specific scenario to protect them from, such as a home invasion or a fire. Remember, harm can come from individuals with malicious intent, acts of nature, or accidental incidents, so "protect from harm" is too vague to work here. Be as specific as possible, and don't worry about predicting all possible scenarios. By the time you are finished with this book, you will be able to think through all possible scenarios you might need to prepare for—but it's impossible to tackle them all at the same time. For now, all that matters is we narrow down the scenario we want to narrowly focus on for this specific SMART goal. As an example, we'll identify the scenario of a home invasion.

"Measurable" dictates the goal must have an established standard and the ability to be tracked. This can be tangible or intangible, with intangible being a little harder to track but can still be measurable. For example, a tangible measure would be to purchase and install a home security system. A nontangible measure would be that all members of your family know and understand your "Home Invasion Safety Plan." Measurable goals are more manageable, as they can be divided up into smaller supporting tasks. (More on supporting tasks in Chapter 4.) No goal is too big, as long as it can be measured. If a goal cannot be measured, you can never be sure if it has been achieved. For example, having a goal of keeping yourself, or others, safe is not measurable. But the methods of how to maintain safety are.

"Attainable" dictates that the goal must be realistic. It would not be realistic to dig a moat around your house as part of your Home Invasion Safety Plan, although I'm sure a lot of you reading would consider that to be an appealing feature to have—me too! However, a more attainable goal would be to put up a fence in the backyard to have a secure private area. This helps prevent us from going on wild goose chases that only end up being a waste of time.

The next principle requires a bit of critical thinking. "Relevant" dictates that the goal must align with your purpose and Core Values identified earlier. In other words, the goal should not be something in which you have no interest; otherwise, you won't be able to make meaningful progress. In my Safety Goals, this is stated as, "To ensure the protection of...myself and my family." This supports my Core Values of safety, security, and family. The Relevant aspect can also specifically relate to a subset of the broader goal, which could be stated as, "To become proficient at hand-to-hand defense methods," or "to become proficient at firearm employment," or "to become proficient at executing our home invasion defense plan," and so on. No matter the details, the important thing is that you can connect your values with your goals somewhere along the line. If you do that, you'll never lose motivation to keep pursuing them.

Lastly, "Timely" dictates that the goal must have an established time frame. The general rule of thumb is that short-term goals can be completed in three months or less, while long-term goals are completed in four months or more. By giving the goal a time frame, you ensure that you are actively thinking of when you can complete it. Otherwise, it may never leave your to-do list.

Below are some examples of SMART Safety Goals, starting with one of my own:

- To ensure protection of my family while at home (Relevant), I will formulate a Home Invasion Safety Plan for my three family members utilizing our current capabilities (Specific, Attainable). The plan will be completed, taught, and known by heart by all family members in one month (Measurable, Timely).

- To ensure the protection of my family while at home, I will formulate a Home Invasion Safety Plan for my four family members utilizing our current capabilities and installing a security system. The plan will be completed, taught, and comprehended by all family members in one month.

- To ensure my protection when getting off work late, I will take weekly hand-to-hand self-defense classes starting next week. I will be able to free myself from anyone's grasp within two months of training.

- To ensure my protection when traveling to Germany, I will review and print off the travel advisories for all my travel locations found at Travel.State.Gov two weeks before I leave for the trip.

Using these Safety Goals, we'll be able to not only define what we want to accomplish in terms of safety, but we'll also gain a greater understanding of ourselves. What do we consider feasible? What is most worth protecting? How do we protect it? Using SMART principles, we'll be able to cut the chaff and get to the heart of who we are, what matters to us, and how we can defend it from harm.

Life Goals

Safety Goals are the definitive end-state solutions that will lead to the ability to focus on your Life Goals. Life Goals are the goals that are at the top of your bucket list—they may even serve as your purpose. For some people, this may be something as big as climbing Mount Everest or as simple as owning a house. As stated before, although this book is about personal safety and self-defense, it is also meant to empower you for the purpose of reaching self-actualization, free from the unmitigated risk of harm. Additionally, having clear Life Goals assists in the proper placement of Safety Goals. If Core Values and Life Goals are two points on a map, Core Values are our starting point, while Life Goals is our destination. A third point, Safety Goals, is a checkpoint placed in between the two points to dictate the easiest route to our destination. Ideally, this route forms a perfectly straight line. With this alignment, it is easier to see and follow a clear direction. If we are missing any one of the points, we will most likely find ourselves wandering aimlessly. Additionally, if our "Safety Goal" checkpoint is located outside of the line formed by the start and end point, there are unnecessary deviations and distances that must be covered to complete the trip. And as we all know, the fastest way to travel is in a straight line.

For those who rely on GPS to get around, consider this your GPS, Goal-oriented Path Selection.

Life Goals follow the same SMART principles as Safety Goals and relate to your personal relationships, career, hobbies, community service, or specific events. Below are a few examples of SMART Life Goals that I and others have used:

- To empower and reach as many people as possible, I will write a book on self-defense, which will be completed by February 15, 2023.
- To save up for a new home, by next year I will save 20 percent of every paycheck, which I will deposit into a savings account. By the end of the year, I should have enough saved for a 20 percent down payment.
- To lose 2 percent body fat in one month, I will eat a minimum of four servings of fruits and vegetables daily and decrease my sugar intake to thirty grams a day. I will plan my meals ahead of time every Sunday and only stock the fridge and pantry with whole, unprocessed foods.
- To improve my cardiovascular health, I will jog a minimum of thirty minutes every Monday, Wednesday, and Friday morning.
- To maintain a healthy relationship with my spouse, I will have at least one conversation a day about something that interests them starting today.
- Starting next month, I will work on nurturing and strengthening my family ties by establishing "family night" on Fridays, where we will

participate in fun games and activities that inspire conversation and camaraderie.

- To increase my knowledge on migration patterns of birds, by July 31st of this year I will read two books, and watch one documentary on the subject.

By this point, you should have identified and built an understanding of your top five Core Values, formulated personal Safety Goals, and developed Life Goals that hopefully will serve as your purpose. Take a minute or two to look over your daily or weekly schedule, or just think back on the last two weeks of your life. Do your current habits align with your values? Are there certain habits that contradict your values?

Don't worry if you don't have all the answers to these questions yet. What matters right now is that you are aware of yourself in a way few are, and soon you'll be able to use that perspective to achieve goals that once seemed impossible.

Chapter 2 Review

Points of Emphasis:

- ❖ Understanding ourselves completely and without bias creates the foundation for personal development and our lives.
- ❖ Core Values are a set of beliefs that embody our personalities, behaviors, and aspirations.

❖ Safety Goals are goals specific to personal protection and self-defense, which provide tangible and intangible measures to ensure safety.

❖ Pursuing Safety Goals fulfills safety needs, allowing you to then pursue Life Goals.

❖ Life Goals are goals specific to your purpose in life. These are your ultimate goals that everything else serves to support. Pursuing and achieving Life Goals brings a sense of happiness, fulfillment, and self-actualization.

❖ When your Core Values, Safety Goals, and Life Goals align, your life is simplified to only what is important to you. You will find you are less stressed, less conflicted, and more motivated.

Perspective:

❖ Being under threat of harm or danger inhibits growth by taking away time, effort, and resources from more pertinent tasks. Being proactive and taking responsibility for your personal safety means you only need to mitigate instances of danger and threats of harm, rather than reacting off-balance. Preparedness will allow you to spend more time on what is important to you.

Call to Action:

☐ Complete the Self-Assessment Worksheet in the CTA Workbook.

Chapter 3:
Strengths and Limitations

"I now know myself to be a person of weakness and strength, liability and giftedness, darkness and light. I now know that to be whole means to reject none of it but to embrace all of it."

Parker J. Palmer

One layer deeper into knowing ourselves is understanding our physical, mental, and emotional capabilities. In this chapter, we will develop an understanding of our strengths and limitations, as well as how they both fit into safety and self-defense strategy. Part of this involves determining whether a skill is a strength or actually a limitation, a surprisingly nuanced task. Facing your own limitations can be difficult for some, but it is important to stay objective, so you do not limit yourself further when it comes to planning and execution. Stay open-minded and go with the flow. If we do this, we'll be able to find where our expertise lies.

We will begin by exploring the three critical elements of what I consider to be the Expertise Criteria. Then, we will learn about strengths and how they provide a foundation for growth. Finally, we will discuss limitations and how they provide opportunity for growth.

Expertise Criteria

My determination of whether a skill is considered to be a strength or limitation is determined by the presence or absence of confidence, efficiency, and pragmatism. These three elements combined are what make up the Expertise Criteria. Tasks that can be done with all three elements of the Expertise Criteria are considered strengths. Tasks that are missing any one of the three elements are considered limitations. Meeting the Expertise Criteria does not necessarily make you an "expert" of the skill; rather, the skill is simply seen as advantageous for you to utilize.

Expertise Criterion 1: Confidence

Confidence is the ability to perform a task with one hundred percent certainty that you can perform the task correctly. When we tie our shoes, there is no second-guessing whether or not we can do it correctly. In fact, we are so confident in our ability to tie our shoes we are normally thinking of other things as we are tying them. This is the amount of confidence needed to consider a skill a true *strength*. Any second-guessing would cause the skill to become a limitation.

Expertise Criterion 2: Efficiency

Efficiency is the next element of determining if a skill is a strength. Efficiency is one's ability to perform a task with appropriate to minimal effort in a relatively timely manner, resulting in the successful completion of said task. Essentially, it is the relationship between the effort exerted and the time it takes to complete a task. "Effort," in these terms, refers to the amount of physical, mental, and emotional exertion used to complete a task. (Yes, emotional effort is a thing, especially in these scenarios. Just think about how it felt in a past argument with a significant other where you felt emotionally drained afterward.) "Timely" refers to the difference between finishing a task within a couple of minutes and finishing the task in a couple of days. It wouldn't make sense for someone to say they are efficient at tying their shoes if it takes them an hour to do so.

Both the effort and the time frame needed to complete a task effectively are usually subjective, as there needs to be an established "standard." Here, our standard is any "average" person—or the individuals in the middle of a normally distributed bell curve, for all you statisticians out there. For example, with our shoe-tying scenario, it takes the "average" person only a couple of minutes or less to complete that task.

Efficiency can also be referred to as "economy of motion." This is a more specific type of efficiency, but it is a concept that will repeat itself throughout this book, and any skill development program. Economy of motion refers to performing a task with the least number of moving parts needed to successfully complete the identified task. When tying our shoes, we normally do not stand on our left foot, lift our right foot to hip height, tie a simple knot on our right foot while balancing in the air, put our right foot down, raise our left foot, tie a simple knot on our left foot while balancing, put down our left foot, raise our right foot, tie a bow, put down our right foot, lift our left foot, tie a bow, put down our left foot, then gleefully start our day. Instead, we bend down to reach our feet, tie a complete knot and bow on one foot, then the other, and then gleefully start our day. This is economy of motion.

No offense is intended to any individual who may tie their shoes in the same manner as the drawn-out example. In fact, if you do, shoot me an email. I'm intrigued.

Expertise Criterion 3: Pragmatism
Lastly, if the solution doesn't solve the problem, the other two elements don't matter. Pragmatism should be the basis for all solutions—we should not do something

if it does not produce the desired results. In this way, it is the most vital of the three. Specific to our concerns, pragmatism does not care if you happen to perform a task differently from what is usually taught or is seen as "the proper way to do it." If you tie your shoe using bunny ears, double knots, or even a square knot with locking knots (for my military readers), it doesn't matter—all that matters is that your shoes stay on your feet. If it works, it works.

Of course, our goal is to combine all three elements, not just one. This will allow us to form strengths where before there were only limitations.

Identifying Strengths and Limitations

Personal strengths are skills, whether physical, mental, emotional, or spiritual, that are performed with all elements of the Expertise Criteria present. A strength may be something you have had for as long as you could remember, like a good memory or quick wit, or something to which you have dedicated time and effort to build your capability, like athletic ability or mental intellect. Strengths will serve as your foundation and motivational tools to get you going and keep you interested when inspiration dwindles. It is human nature to lose interest in an activity if we are not good at it or do not understand it, therefore; strengths will be the bridge to rehabilitating limitations if need be. Kind of like dipping healthy, tasteless food into ranch so it is more appealing to eat. Hey, I'm from the south, and we put ranch on everything.

Limitations are skills, whether physical, mental, emotional, or spiritual, that are performed with one or more of the elements of the Expertise Criteria missing. Usually, limitations are skills and tasks we have neglected, never needed, or actively hide from. Some limitations do not affect our overall ability to perform. Others cause deviations in strategy and performance. For example, if we have a left ankle injury, we would be forced to limp and rely on our right leg more than usual to keep us standing and moving. This would be okay for a little while, but by focusing more on the right leg and neglecting the left, we can cause a shift in our posture that, if left for too long, will start to cause lingering effects. Before we know it, we have a right-leaning gait, with strong right-side muscle groups and weaker left-side muscle groups. By not providing a rehabilitating solution to the physical limitation, it may cause unwanted adaptations and result in more work for us (or simply more limitations) in the long run.

Our goal is to identify relevant limitations that are causing unwanted adaptations and to then develop rehabilitative solutions so that there are no lingering negative effects. Note: not all limitations are relative to our focus here, as we are only concerned with limitations that, if persistent, would create a hindrance in your ability to fulfill your Safety Goals. For example, one of my limitations is that I cannot fly an airplane. This does not translate into a disadvantage or produce any negative effects relating to my Safety Goals or aspirations, as flying an airplane has no relation to my lifestyle. As a result, it's much more pragmatic to ignore that limitation. A more relative limitation would be if I was not able to drive all the vehicles within my household—for example, if I could not drive a vehicle with a manual transmission. This limitation could end up causing negative effects during a Safety Event if a situation arises where I needed to drive said vehicle to get my family away from a threat. Due to my current lack of efficiency and lack of confidence, learning to operate all household vehicles should be considered and addressed.

At this point, you should understand the process of identifying and evaluating your current abilities and capabilities by utilizing Expertise Criteria. Only when a skill is performed confidently, efficiently, and pragmatically should it be implemented into a formulated Safety Plan, which we will develop in Section Three. With that said, if a skill is considered to be vital to a Safety Plan with no practical alternatives, that skill should be developed no matter the current expertise level. For example, performing CPR and first aid is vital to any Safety Plan. Even if you have no experience in the medical field, basic medical skills are vital and should be developed. The goal is to build on strengths while working to rehabilitate or mitigate limitations. Once we have done that, we can develop our plan with the confidence, efficiency, and pragmatism needed to make it successful.

Chapter 3 Review

Points of Emphasis:

- ❖ The Expertise Criteria is a set of three principles needed for a skill to be considered a strength. The three principles are: confidence, efficiency, and pragmatism.
    - ➢ Confidence is the ability to perform a task with one hundred percent certainty you can complete it successfully.
    - ➢ Efficiency is the ability to perform the task with the minimum required effort in a timely manner.
    - ➢ Pragmatism is knowing how to take a practical, logical, and effective approach to a problem set.
- ❖ Strengths are skills that can be performed with all three Expertise Criteria present. Limitations are skills that are missing one or more of the required three elements.

Perspective:

❖ We all have different strengths and limitations. Ideally, we would be able to negate all our limitations and turn them into strengths. This is not realistic. Therefore, we must strategize to maximize our strengths and lessen our limitations so we can play by our rules.

Call to Action:

☐ Answer the following questions.

    ☐ What do you consider to be your Strengths?

    ☐ Do they meet each of the three elements in the Expertise Criterion?

    ☐ What do you consider to be your Limitations?

    ☐ What element(s) are missing within the Expertise Criterion?

Chapter 4:
Curriculum, Programming, and Skill Development

"I hated every minute of training, but I said, 'Don't quit. Suffer now and live the rest of your life as a champion.'"

Muhammad Ali

Now that we have our foundation, we can begin building a curriculum. Skills and abilities can be developed without a systematic detailed program; however, without programming, the process is usually riddled with trial and error, unnecessary setbacks, and inconsistent or unmeasurable progress. It's like having a sports team with no coach. With set programming, one can maintain a schedule, track progress, mitigate burnout, and tailor one's training to their individual needs and capability. A developmental program is the means to an end, the definable pathway needed to reach your goal.

The elements and steps to creating and following a sound training program are:

1. Isolate one SMART goal.
2. Divide that one SMART goal into multiple supporting tasks.
3. Utilize backward planning.
4. Complete an initial assessment.
5. Monitor and track progress.

We will soon go through each of these steps one by one—however, if this is a completely new concept, there might be growing pains while you try to develop a program. You may not be able to develop a full training program and may need to adopt a program from a third party. This is completely fine. Nevertheless, if you practice the methodology in this chapter, you will have a better understanding of training as a whole, which will allow you to better vet third party programs and ultimately take more responsibility for your training and development.

As any professional athlete can tell you, the difference between good and great is the application of a structured program. Athleticism has basically become a science. Every skill drill, training session, and individual exercise performed by professional athletes has been formulated to produce precise desired results at optimal levels. This is why different positions on a football team conduct different training sessions—they're focusing on different skills. It's not just in sports—education follows the same model, as education curriculums are built to increase comprehension while enabling practical application of the subject. The military implements performance-based training, which follows designed programs tailored for military-specific tasks. Businesses use developmental programs for on-the-job training, employee development, and business development. In short, everyone and their mama is using designed programs to learn skills, develop individuals, and optimize performance. Why wouldn't we do it for safety and self-defense?

1. Isolate a Goal

By now, you should have a conceptual understanding of SMART goals and how they are used. If you have multiple Safety Goals, here you should isolate each one individually to begin dividing each goal into supporting tasks. To avoid confusion, only work on creating one program/curriculum per goal at a time. I would recommend starting with a Safety Goal that provides comprehensive security (e.g., goals relating to a home invasion or active shooter), as it will provide basic safety across the board while you work on some of your more specific goals. Alternatively, you could also choose to start with a goal that pertains to an ongoing situation you are currently dealing with. No matter how you prioritize or which goal you begin with first, each goal will be evaluated and developed in the same manner. In this example, we will review the steps on the following SMART goal pertaining to first aid:

"In order to save the life of my family members during a trauma medical emergency, I will learn how to provide basic emergency first aid in one month."

2. Create Supporting Tasks

Next, we must analyze the goal itself to identify its supporting tasks and accompanying skills. Supporting tasks are tasks that you are required to complete in order to be able to achieve the SMART goal; the accompanying skills are the skills necessary to perform each supporting task. Yes, it is a bit of a Russian nesting doll situation, where each element provides a bridge to the next that ultimately produces a comprehensive effect. It's recommended to identify no more than five supporting tasks per goal, as any more than that may take up too much of your time. Each supporting task will need its own curriculum or training program, which may or may not be interconnected with the others.

It is possible that these supporting tasks are already written into your goal. For example, the goal, "To ensure the protection of myself when getting off work late, I will take weekly hand-to-hand self-defense classes starting next week, and I will be able to free myself from anyone's grasp within two months of training," already identifies the supporting task of taking lessons in hand-to-hand combat. Additionally, we could also conclude that strength and cardiovascular fitness are accompanying skills, as hand-to-hand combat requires a certain level of fitness to perform efficiently.

Other times, you may *not* have supporting tasks already written into your Safety Goal. In the case of creating and implementing a Home Invasion Safety Plan, there are many ways to approach this. A simple "how to..." internet search can provide a good start when researching a topic and identifying supporting tasks. Some examples of supporting tasks when it comes to Home Invasion Safety Plan may include learning first aid, firearm employment, gadget operation, de-escalation and communication, combatives, and basic fitness. You also, perhaps, may have to complete supporting tasks that are less tangible, such as research development or educating yourself on criminology concepts.

Below are the identified supporting tasks in our Safety Goal, "In order to save the life of my family members during a trauma medical emergency, I will learn how to provide basic emergency first aid in one month.":

- Become certified in CPR.
- Learn how to bandage a wound.
- Learn how to use basic medical equipment.
- Learn basic anatomy.

3. Backward Planning

Once all supporting tasks are identified, the general training program is formulated through backward planning—in other words, start with the end goal, and plan achievable steps leading back to a start point. Instead of planning in an order of Step 1, Step 2, Step 3, and so on, we plan in reverse order of overall goal, Step 3, Step 2, Step 1. Backward planning for buying a soda from a vending machine is, Step 4: Grab soda from vending machine slot, Step 3: Choose the type of soda, Step 2: Insert money into the vending machine, Step 1: Go to a vending machine.

The overall goal of backward planning ensures you create a comprehensive and progressive training program, as it forces you to ask yourself, "What is needed beforehand to achieve this task?" You know you have covered all the bases when you ask yourself that question and you already have the ability to achieve that particular task. Kids are great at this, since when a child asks you over and over, "But why?", they are forcing you to think through a process similar to backward planning. Hopefully, this will be an easier process than explaining to a child where babies come from.

Backward planning is only concerned with major movements and broad concepts. All the details will be added later, once there is a clear start and finish. I recommend using backward planning to formulate three distinct levels of training: fundamental concepts, practical application, and tailored solutions.

1. **Fundamental concepts** are all applicable theories, concepts, and teachings that provide the foundational understanding of the practical skill or knowledge. These are the basic building blocks needed to understand and implement a skill. Think simple. As an example, when learning math, you started with addition, subtraction, multiplication, and division. In our example, fundamental concepts include understanding anatomy and pathology, or the types of injuries.

2. **Practical application** is the general real-world application of the skill or knowledge beyond theory and conceptual instruction. These are the "hands-on" physical actions that are part of the skill set. Fundamental math can be applied to engineering, finances, physics, etc. In our example, practical application is conducting CPR and applying treatment, such as a bandage or splint.

3. **Tailored solutions** are the implementation of the skills or knowledge that fits your specific goals at the moment. Tailored solutions are the individual skills that bridge formalized training to the supporting tasks. These are the skills used

to enable the achievement of your Safety Goals and the satisfaction of your individual needs. Physics can be applied to firearms training and understanding bullet trajectory of a firearm you may own, and engineering can be applied to installing a new security system in your home. In our example, the tailored solution is the ability to provide first aid to my specific family members who are a two-year-old and thirty-five-year-old.

Following the directions of backward planning, you would start by establishing clear objectives of 3) tailored solutions, then 2) practical application, and lastly, 1) fundamental concepts.

Below are three examples of backward planning including our first aid training example. The key here is to understand the distinct purpose for each level of training, the types of objectives within each level, and how each level connects to the next.

Firearms Training Backward Planning Example:
- Tailored Solutions
    - Engage one target at a range of 5–10 meters in a dark environment with a 9mm pistol from behind cover.
    - Engage multiple targets at a range of 5–10 meters in a lighted environment with a 9mm pistol.

- Practical Application
  - Tactical Skills
    - Live fire reloads drills
    - Weapon malfunction drills
    - Moving from cover to cover
  - Advanced Marksmanship
    - Target engagement behind cover
    - Low-light target engagement with flashlight
- Fundamental Concepts
  - Basic Marksmanship Skills
    - Dry-fire drills
    - Static engagement of targets at 5–25 meters
  - General Operation Skills
    - Pistol components and functions
    - Clearing procedures and functions check
  - Weapon Safety
    - Firearm safety principles
    - Firearm storage methods

Combatives Backward Planning Example:
- Tailored Solutions
  - Escaping when an individual grabs me from behind while standing.
  - Escaping when an individual pins me to the ground.

- Practical Application
  - Mount escape techniques
  - Guard retention to sweep techniques
  - Takedown defense techniques
- Fundamental Concepts
  - Basic positions and stances
  - Basic strikes and attacks
  - Basic strike defense

Emergency First Aid Backward Planning Example:

- Tailored Solutions
  - Utilizing the equipment in the family first aid bag, provide first aid to my two-year-old daughter.
  - Utilizing the equipment in the family first aid bag, provide first aid to my thirty-five-year-old spouse.
- Practical Application
  - Cardiopulmonary Resuscitation (CPR)
    - One rescuer
    - Two rescuers
    - Pediatric patient
    - Adult patient
  - Hemorrhage Control
    - Use and application of a tourniquet
    - Wrapping and bandaging techniques

- Bone Fractures
  - Arm splinting techniques
  - Leg splinting techniques
- Fundamental Concepts
  - Anatomy and Physiology
    - Pediatric
    - Adult
    - Geriatric
  - Traumatic Injury Pathology
    - Head injuries
    - Blunt force trauma
    - Lacerations/bleeding
    - Respiratory issues
    - Hypothermia

Once backward planning is completed, you simply reverse the order, and you have the general outline for your training program/curriculum. Below is our general training program/curriculum for our SMART goal, "In order to save the life of my family members during a trauma medical emergency, I will learn how to provide emergency first aid in one month.":

- Fundamental Concepts
  - Anatomy and Physiology
    - Pediatric
    - Adult
    - Geriatric

- ○ Traumatic Injury Pathology
    - Head injuries
    - Blunt force trauma
    - Lacerations/bleeding
    - Respiratory issues
    - Hypothermia
- Practical Application
    - ○ Cardiopulmonary Resuscitation (CPR)
        - One rescuer
        - Two rescuers
        - Pediatric patient
        - Adult patient
    - ○ Hemorrhage Control
        - Use and application of a tourniquet
        - Wrapping and bandaging techniques
    - ○ Bone Fractures
        - Arm splinting techniques
        - Leg splinting techniques
- Tailored Solutions
    - ○ Utilizing the equipment in the family first aid bag, provide first aid to my two-year-old daughter.
    - ○ Utilizing the equipment in the family first aid bag, provide first aid to my thirty-five-year-old spouse.

Isn't it nice to have everything organized in front of you? A lot of people are intimidated by Safety Goals because of all they have to do. It can be overwhelming. But with a proper program, you can shrink it to a manageable size.

4. Initial Assessment

Once you have created or found a program that fits your needs, it is important to conduct an initial assessment of each supporting task. An initial assessment is the first test of a skill or knowledge, and it serves three purposes:

1. The first is to give you exposure to the content. Knowing is half the battle, so this is a chance to expose yourself to the subject material to better understand it.
2. The second is to manage your expectations. Usually, we believe a new task will be impossible to achieve or that we are a natural-born expert. Both are counterproductive, as unrealistic expectations can lead to unnecessary adversity or loss of motivation.
3. The third purpose is to provide a foundational metric to track and compare your progress—this is the true value of the initial assessment.

In our example, an initial timed assessment of applying a bandage on a pretend open wound on an arm can measure the efficiency and pragmatism of applying a bandage. The time completed and whether or not the bandage stays secure in place would be the foundational metric to compare ourselves to in subsequent assessments.

Note: depending on the skill, the initial assessment should not be a test of the tailored solutions you identified during your planning, as it may be dangerous and/or too demanding for a novice. In our first aid example, the tailored solution involves providing emergency first aid to a two-year-old. As such, applying an effective tourniquet—a device that completely cuts off blood flow to an extremity—would cause unnecessary pain and harm to the child. It should go without saying, but I'll say it: applying a tourniquet on a child or individuals with clotting disorders outside of a medical emergency is not advised. Instead, it's recommended for the initial assessment to address the *fundamental* concepts. If the supporting task requires a physical action, you may need to seek a trainer or professional to assist in facilitating the initial assessment. If the supporting task is more knowledge-based, you may find relevant tests or quizzes online that could serve as the initial assessment. An internet search of "basic (insert skill) test/quiz" will usually provide a few. If your training involves weaponry, all training with the physical weapon should be conducted under the supervision of a trained professional and/or medical professional.

5. *Monitor and Track Progress*

An effective program will produce measurable progress in an appropriate amount of time. To ensure this, we'll self-monitor and ensure that any program we use follows a model of progressive stress. Here, we are not using the usual definition of stress—as in being "stressed out." Rather, we are using "stress" as defined by Hans Selye as "the non-specific response of the body to any demand for change"[1]—such as your body's response while reading this book. Progressive stress is the gradual introduction of stimuli that, in turn, will cause gradual response and progress. Hopefully, reading this book provides just enough stress that it forces your mind to think through the concepts it introduces,

thereby increasing your knowledge and under-standing of the subject. If instead your brain feels like mush, then you should read and digest the material at a slower pace. Adding too much demand too rapidly can cause discouragement as well as threat of harm or injury, as is the case with physical demand.

---

1 "What Is Stress?" The American Institute of Stress, January 4, 2017, https://www.stress.org/what-is-stress.

Additionally, tracking progress provides continuous motivation to sustain a program. We are more likely to stick with a program when we see positive results. Conversely, if no progress is shown, the current program should be modified or an entirely new program should be implemented. I have found success in tracking my progress by keeping a handwritten journal and updating it after each training session with the type of skill trained; quantitative information, such as score totals, recorded times, and measurable drill parameters; and qualitative information, such as overall energy level, cognitive clarity during the session, and motivation level. If you are more of a tech-person, keeping a spreadsheet or notes on your smartphone may be more convenient. Note: some skills and abilities take more time to develop than others, so measurable progress is relative to the skill. A great example of that is almost all fitness programs. Fitness progress is usually subtle. More than likely, any improvements will be noticed by others before you notice them yourself. Be patient, stick with it, and remember to keep your expectations realistic. Any progress is progress.

There are hundreds of established training programs available you can utilize. I recommend following these steps of curriculum and program development, so if you do decide to go with an existing program, you are able to align it with the plan you have created. Not all programs are created equal, and not all programs fit every individual. The key is developing and finding a program that is designed for your needs.

Now that you have created your Safety Goal, identified supporting tasks, discovered their accompanying skills, and produced a program to develop those skills, you have done all the preparatory work needed to take action.

Essentially, this is the decisive point. In the military, a "decisive point" is a geographic place, specific key event, critical system, or function that allows commanders to gain a marked advantage over an enemy and greatly influence the outcome of an attack. It is basically the "no going back" point. And there is no reason to go back, as you have too much potential to stop now. Taking control of your safety and your life is too important to just think about. It's time to put the plan into action.

It's time to reach your full potential.

Chapter 4 Review

Points of Emphasis:

❖ Education and skill development is better facilitated when following a systematic program and curriculum respectively.

❖ Program and curriculum development can be done in a five-step process:

1. Identify one SMART goal.

2. Create up to five supporting tasks.

3. Backward plan for each supporting task development, from tailored solutions to practical application to fundamental concepts.

4. Conduct an initial assessment.

5. Implement the program and track your progress.

Perspective:

❖ Education and skill development is not a straightforward process. It is a journey of good days and not-so-good days. But one thing is certain: it is rewarding and will pay dividends. No matter your age, height, weight, race, gender, socioeconomic status, or education level (or insert infinite demographic types here), personal development and growth is *the* means to a more fulfilling life, no matter the subject.

Call to Action:

☐ Complete the Program/Curriculum Development Worksheet in the CTA Workbook.

Chapter 5:
Sport Psychology and Optimal Performance

"Being relaxed, at peace with yourself, confident, emotionally neutral, loose, and free-floating—these are the keys to successful performance in almost everything."

Dr. Wayne W. Dyer

Reaching your full potential is much more than just going through the motions. We don't want to be just mediocre or competent in a task or skill; we want to excel and be the best at what we do. We want to be confident, efficient, and pragmatic, especially if what we are doing is protecting the well-being of ourselves and our loved ones. The old saying used to go, "Practice makes perfect," but we now understand that practice makes habit, whether perfect or not. Research conducted in the field of sports psychology helps fine-tune performance measures so your practice and real-world implementation will be as close to perfect as possible.

Sports psychology is the study of psychological factors that influence physical performance, such as arousal, confidence, and attention focus. Although primarily used for sports performance, the principles and research from this field can and should be applied to everyday tasks, and especially to the tasks and principles outlined in this book. Specifically, we will review performance-enhancing methodology that can be applied when training and performing individual skills and complete scenarios. This includes focus training, visualization, and the concept of being "in the zone."

Focus Training

Focus training is the practice of relaxation and distraction awareness. It essentially allows you to focus and stay focused despite any distractions that may pop up (Checked your phone recently?). The benefit of focus training is the *conscious* link it creates between thoughts and physiological systems. There is already an *un*conscious link between thoughts and physiological systems, whether the effect is negative or positive. Relating to self-defense scenarios, when exposed to stress, our body naturally increases its heart rate and breathing—we might begin to sweat, and our muscles might tense. This causes our thoughts to become erratic, hazy, and irregular, which in turn makes it more difficult to execute our normal decision-making process. Focus training acts to reverse this unconscious occurrence through conscious practice, leading to controllable mitigation. It combines breath control with the ability to actively maintain concentration through awareness.

Believe it or not, focus training was a part of my training to become a medic. War can be pretty distracting, and if your job is to provide life-saving treatment to a wounded individual, it is best you stay focused. So I can say firsthand that these practices do what they are supposed to do.

And yes, focus training is essentially meditation. However, you do not need to find a mountaintop and sit cross-legged, with a dramatic, panoramic, cinematic shot of wind blowing through your hair to meditate. In fact, in the case of military medics, the scene is much more chaotic and far less relaxing. That said, although meditation could be helpful for your overall health and stress reduction, for our purposes, I would like for you to think of this as training rather than a meditation practice.

But how do we train ourselves to relax enough to focus? Mindful breathing is the simplest and single most effective method for relaxation and boosting performance. Need to decrease your heart rate? Control your breathing. Need to lower your blood pressure? Control your breathing. Need to save yourself from losing your job because you are about to tell your boss off? Control your breathing. Although breathing is mostly an autonomous function of the body, it is the one vital sign we actively have control over—hence why it is the key variable to affect all other vital functions. Breathing helps regulate the chemicals of oxygen and carbon dioxide in the body. If our quality of breath is decreased, the balance of oxygen and carbon dioxide is altered, causing physiological and mental effects throughout our bodies and minds. Therefore, quality of breath is the foundation of focus training. The standard principles of mindful breathing include slowly inhaling through your nose for five to six seconds, ensuring expansion of your stomach and not your chest, holding for one second, and exhaling either through your nose or mouth for three to four seconds. It's important to breathe through the belly, called diaphragmatic breathing, as it enables complete expansion of the lungs and overall area for gas exchange. Eventually, you'll be able to focus completely on your breath, your body, and your surroundings without getting distracted.

Distraction awareness is actually the byproduct of the goal of complete focus. However, since complete focus can only be maintained for a short period of time, the goal naturally becomes increasing your awareness when distractions arise. The Mackworth Clock Test, a psychological experiment, has shown that even the most disciplined professionals can only maintain complete focus on a specific task for a period of time before constant and continual decline. During the experiment, radar technicians were asked to monitor a clock-like device in which a light would travel around a circle similar to how the minute hand travels around a clock. The light would randomly perform "double jumps" where the radar technician performing the experiment would press a button in acknowledgment of the "double jump." The study showed the performance of the radar technician would decrease upward of 15 percent within the first half hour alone, with performance decreasing furthermore as time progressed.[2] By the way, during that time, radar technicians' main job outside of the experiment was to monitor the radar screen to track blobs of light passing through a circular screen. They were essentially the pros of attention and vigilance, but even *they* fell prey to distractions.

When beginning a focus practice, you will likely find that you are distracted more than you maintain focus. This is normal yet still frustrating. The good news is it does provide you with a starting point to build upon. The aim is not to completely block out distractions, as relevant research shows this to be impossible. The aim is to gain awareness of when you are distracted as quickly as possible so you can refocus on the task at hand. You can even start practicing distraction awareness while you are reading this book. As you read, notice any times

---

2 N. H. Mackworth, "The Breakdown of Vigilance during Prolonged Visual Search," *Quarterly Journal of Experimental Psychology* 1, no. 1 (1948): 6–21, https://doi.org/10.1080/17470214808416738.

you become distracted, or any moments when you didn't fully comprehend the information as you read it. When that happens, take a brief moment to practice mindful breathing, and then return to the book. By the time you finish the book, you will have already established your focus baseline, meaning you should have a good idea of how often and for how long you usually become distracted, while also developing a useful skill for eliminating distraction and refocusing.

Visualization

Visualization is the practice of mentally envisioning performing a task perfectly. Notice I said perfectly, as what we see is what we do. Visualization can be used for a single skill or—as we will go over in a later chapter—an entire plan. One of its biggest benefits is that it can be performed anywhere, such as lying in bed, riding in a car, or before an athletic event, to name a few. Many studies have shown that visualization, also known as imagery, activates the same neural pathways as physically performing the visualized task.[3] Simply put, your body's nervous system acts similar to when you actually land a slama-jama knockout punch when you are just imagining it. This is noteworthy considering we do not have the time or resources to physically train 24/7.

---

3 Th. Mulder, "Motor Imagery and Action Observation: Cognitive Tools for Rehabilitation," *Journal of Neural Transmission* 114, no. 10 (2007): 1265–78, https://doi.org/10.1007/s00702-007-0763-z.

Instead, we can use visualization throughout our busy day and still effectively train neurological pathways.

The other key component of visualization, rather than just the visualization of the mechanics, is the associated verbal cues. Verbal cues are summary phrases that provide focus during a task, such as "keep your eye on the ball," "keep hips square," "front sight post," and "breathe." Notice that none of these verbal cues start with "don't." This is a common mistake and should be avoided. When you construct a verbal cue with "don't," you are actually focusing on the action you do *not* want to perform. Your mind doesn't differentiate between do and don't; it is just *do*. So, when you say things like, "don't look down," or "don't cross your feet," your mind is actually focused on looking down or crossing your feet. Therefore, ensure that any verbal cues you create are focused on the action you want to actually "do."

"In the Zone"

Being "in the zone" is scientifically known as being in "a state of flow." This refers to the state of performing a task with complete focus, control, and enjoyment. Athletes normally describe this as a state of instinctively knowing what is happening and what will happen while feeling as if it is all happening in slow motion. This is often where they play the best, or at least feel the most comfortable during a close game. It is my belief that the enjoyment aspect is the key element to being "in the zone." I cannot say I have ever been "in the zone" when doing something I didn't like, and I would bet that is the case for you too. Admittedly, the enjoyment aspect will not necessarily be present during a Safety Event, unless you are in fact an adrenaline junkie.

It is my theory that being "in the zone" is being in a state of focused problem-solving. This is done by identifying problems before they become problems and knowing how to solve them instantaneously. This, of course, can only happen after constant exposure, usually in the form of training, practice, and real-world experience. For example, when first introduced to tic-tac-toe, the game seemed difficult, and you really had to think about your (and your opponent's) next moves carefully. However, through practice, you began to predict the opponent's moves and were able to make moves to force your opponent into marking the boxes you wanted them to mark. This is the type of focused problem-solving I am referring to that happens "in the zone."

(By the way, marking the center box on the first turn counteracts those who use the corner "triple threat" strategy.)

Focus training, visualization, and being "in the zone" are not the only aspects of sports psychology that could be helpful in developing protection techniques, but these are the basis for any training, and can also serve as practice for improved life management. The concepts in the previous chapter established a step-by-step blueprint that will lead you to accomplishing your Safety Goals. The principles introduced in this chapter ensure you are optimizing each training session, as well as developing practical conditioning needed for a Safety Event. Using a program carefully designed to work for you, by you, will help you prepare, predict, and visualize everything you might need to achieve your Safety and Life Goals.

Chapter 5 Review

Points of Emphasis:

- ❖ Focus training, which includes distraction awareness and mindful breathing, improves your ability to focus on important factors relevant to a specific task without irrelevant distractions.
- ❖ Visualization, also known as imagery, and associated verbal cues increase motor efficiency by training the connection between mind and body.
- ❖ Being "in the zone" refers to the natural flow between mind and body when deeply engaged with a specific task. This state is accomplished through complete familiarization and enjoyment of the task.

Perspective:

- ❖ There is nothing fun about going through a Safety Event. It is stressful beyond comprehension, physically exhausting, and mentally draining. However, skills that improve survivability in Safety Events—such as learning martial arts—can be enjoyable. Hopefully, they will turn into hobbies that you'll maintain throughout your life. If so, the principles of this chapter will help you in mastering those skills, as well as any other skills you seek to master to achieve your Life Goals.

Call to Action:

- ☐ Implement a one-minute focus training session as a part of your daily routine. Set a timer and practice mindful breathing and maintaining focus on your five senses. When you find yourself distracted, bring yourself back to your breath by counting the seconds of your inhales and exhales. Once you are comfortable with one minute, you can increase your sessions for as long as you need.
- ☐ Implement a one-minute visualization training session as a part of your daily routine. Set a timer and visualize yourself performing a task that supports a Safety Goal. Ensure it is done in your mind without mistakes. Increase the session duration as needed. Repeat as needed.

Chapter 6:
Preparedness vs. Obsession

"Obsession is just another round on the merry-go-round of unfinished business."

Dale Andrews

A s the story of Goldilocks tells us, too little or too much of something is never a good thing. This holds true regarding preparedness for instances of self-protection and the protection of others. There's a fine line between preparedness and obsession—being too prepared can harm you in the long run, creating an environment of paranoia, stress, fear, and unhealthy fixation. Conversely, there is also risk—far too much risk—in not being prepared. Too little effort in taking responsibility for your safety leaves you vulnerable to harm and reliant on others to provide that safety.

Since you are reading this book, I know you are convinced of the importance of preparedness. Therefore, the purpose of this chapter is to advise caution when exploring the subjects and methodology of safety and self-defense. We will look at the difference between preparedness and obsession, the signs and symptoms of obsession, and how to prevent obsessive behavior.

As I am writing this book, my wife and I happen to be looking for a new daycare provider for our daughter. In this time of uncertainty and new challenges, this chapter is really hitting home, not so much because of the legwork of finding and selecting a provider, but because of all the "what if's" and potential scenarios that could arise. After all, it's not ideal to allow a complete stranger to watch and care for your child. There are too many variables, too many risks, and no way to mitigate them all. Will they be as vigilant as I am while caring for my child? Do they have Safety Plans in place for certain scenarios? Is there a possibility that they themselves are an insider threat?

I am having to take a dose of my own medicine by maintaining a level of preparedness without crossing the line into obsession. Specifically, I am exhibiting the symptom of doubt and having difficulty tolerating uncertainty—which I will note later as one of the many signs of obsession. Currently, this is my only symptom, and since I am aware of it, I am able to prevent it from becoming more severe. But you can see how it would be easy for me to allow myself to sink into an unhealthy state of obsession. As you will see, obsession is not always the movie dramatization state of a "crazy person" drawing pictures on the wall; rather, it is a subtle, persistent creep that causes drastic changes in behavior when left unchecked.

Defined by New Oxford American Dictionary, preparedness is "a state of readiness,"[4] while obsession is "an idea or thought that continually preoccupies or intrudes on a person's mind."[5] When compared, it is clear that preparedness is a conscious, deliberate effort, while obsession is the state of uncontrolled impulses. Preparedness has a defined end state, like our Safety Goals—although subjective, a state of readiness can be clearly defined. As such, once the goal has been accomplished, the action can be modified for maintenance or adjusted for the next goal. In other words, preparedness consists of deliberate actions taken in measurable steps to reach a state of predetermined readiness for a specified event.

Obsession, within the subject matter of this book, can manifest in one of two ways: from the fear of violence or from the intense interest in the methodology of self-defense and personal protection.

Fear may turn into a phobia, leading to unceasing anxiety, which may cause drastic changes in thoughts

---

4 "preparedness," In *New Oxford American Dictionary*, edited by Stevenson, Angus, and Christine A. Lindberg. : Oxford University Press, 2010, https://www-oxfordreference-com.ezproxy.umgc.edu/view/10.1093/acref/9780195392883.001.0001/m_en_us1280408.

5 "obsession," In *New Oxford American Dictionary*, edited by Stevenson, Angus, and Christine A. Lindberg. : Oxford University Press, 2010, https://www-oxfordreference-com.ezproxy.umgc.edu/view/10.1093/acref/9780195392883.001.0001/m_en_us1272710.

and behavior. Viktor Frankl, a renowned psychiatrist and Holocaust survivor, theorized on what he referred to as *anticipatory anxiety*. Dr. Frankl described anticipatory anxiety as fearing an event or situation so much "that it produces precisely that of which the patient is afraid".[6] In this case, anxiety might not actually lead to a random stranger breaking into your house or a stalker magically appearing when you are walking alone at night. However, even if the situation does not manifest itself in reality, just thinking about the feared event occurring can create a similar, if not the same, psychological response as if it did happen in reality. So, if I think of a scenario where a masked figure assaults me while walking to my car in the middle of the night, my mental, emotional, and even physical response will be the same as it would be if it actually happened. Subsequently, it may create real change in the way I think or perceive a real situation due to the imaginary event.

Conversely, obsession based on interest likely begins innocently enough—as curiosity, progressing into overwhelming interest, leading to indulgence and uncontrolled habits. The issue arises when the thought patterns and habits that are formed are created by a nondeliberate, subconscious drive. Hobbies and training are not usually seen as obsessions, as they

---

6 Viktor E. Frankl, Harold S. Kushner, and William J. Winslade, Man's search for meaning (Boston, MA: Beacon Press, 2006), 173, Apple Books.

follow intentional and deliberate motivations and actions. But issues can arise when there is exposure to an unhealthy or negative influence on a hobby or preexisting habit. This is the case when athletes turn to unhealthy training practices—such as drastic weight loss methods or abusing performance-enhancing drugs—when looking to gain a competitive advantage.

The key in preventing obsessive behavior is recognizing the problem before it turns into an unconscious habit, or compulsion. Obsessive-compulsive disorder, commonly referred to as OCD, is the medical diagnosis one is given when obsessive thoughts interfere with one's life and daily habits. Since it is a condition that must be diagnosed by a medical professional, here we can only speak to the correlation between obsessive thoughts and the changed behavior it creates. Once obsessive behavior escalates to the point of compulsive habit, it takes a lot of effort, and usually professional help, to rehabilitate. Preventing obsessive behavior is manageable through gaining awareness of the issue, understanding the root cause(s), and developing habits that divert your attention away from the root cause(s). Yes, it is easier said than done. However, this process also sounds similar to other processes we have implemented in other spaces, namely problem-solving and awareness training.

As I stated before, self-awareness is an important quality to have, and it is also the hardest to perfect. As the saying goes, "We don't know what we don't know," so when we are introduced to a particular subject we may not even be aware that the behavior is harmful. For that reason, I want to provide information that may help distinguish between behaviors that are productive and those that are harmful. Although correlated with OCD, the following are signs and symptoms that are specific to obsession, as provided by the Mayo Clinic:[7]

- Doubting and having difficulty tolerating uncertainty.
- Aggressive or horrific thoughts about losing control and harming yourself or others.
- Unwanted thoughts, including aggression, or sexual or religious subjects.
- Intense stress when objects aren't orderly.
- Avoidance of situations that can trigger obsessions.

Exhibiting one sign or symptom shouldn't be much cause for concern. However, when exhibiting multiple signs and symptoms, it's recommended to at least speak to a family member, friend, or a medical professional about the specific sign(s) or symptom(s). That's not to say a person is automatically deemed an

7 Mayo Clinic Staff, "Obsessive-Compulsive Disorder (OCD)," Mayo Clinic, Mayo Foundation for Medical Education and Research, March 11, 2020, https://www.mayoclinic.org/diseases-conditions/obsessive-compulsive-disorder/symptoms-causes/syc-20354432.

obsessive person if exhibiting any of these traits. Only, that a conversation might be enough to relieve any concern(s), worry, stress, or anxiety.

Conversely, it is important to be able to identify when a hobby or activity becomes harmful to aspects of our lives, whether health, family, work, and so on. Behavioral addiction is a topic debated within the medical community, but the focus here is understanding when an activity is doing more harm than good. According to the article, "Phenomenology and Treatment of Behavioural Addictions", "behavior addictions are characterized by an inability to resist an urge or drive resulting in actions that are harmful to oneself or others."[8] The key phrase being "knowledge of adverse consequences," since if we aren't aware of the adverse effects, then we are less likely to fix the issue. To help with that, I have found a list of signs and symptoms to look out for. According to AddictionResource.net, the signs and symptoms of behavioral addictions are:[9]

- Having the majority of your life revolve around the behavior.
- Feeling a 'buzz' or 'high' after engaging in the behavior.

8   Jon E. Grant, Liana RN Schreiber, and Brian L Odlaug. "Phenomenology and Treatment of Behavioural Addictions," *The Canadian Journal of Psychiatry* 58, no. 5 (2013): 252–59, https://doi.org/10.1177/070674371305800502.

9   Addiction Resource Editorial Staff, "Behavioral Addictions: Causes, Signs, and Treatment Options," Addiction Resource, August 10, 2021, https://www.addictionresource.net/behavioral-addictions/.

- Feeling a need to engage in the behavior more often over time.
- Continuing to engage in a behavior despite negative consequences to health, social life, relationships, or other personal conflicts.
- Neglecting work or school to engage in the behavior.
- Feeling unable to cut down on or stop the behavior.
- Denying you have a problem or minimizing its harms.
- Becoming hostile or angry when confronted about the compulsive behavior.
- Experiencing signs of withdrawal (e.g., anxiety, depression, fatigue) if you try to stop engaging in the compulsive behavior.

If the root cause of obsession stems from worry or fear, speaking to others will create a broader sense of awareness and perspective. This is helpful in cases where our fears and anxieties are exacerbated by our skewed or narrow perspective of a subject. Conversely, if the root cause stems from extreme interest, speaking with others can help refocus our attention to tasks or responsibilities regarded as meaningful and relevant to our lives.

Asking for support when it's needed isn't a sign of weakness; it is a sign of strength. In my experience, it is not easy to proactively seek aid. The thought of opening up to others brings a dose of harsh reality and uncertainty on how others will perceive the issue at hand. The reality is the environment created after seeking aid is never one of judgment, persecution, humiliation, or harm. Rather, it fosters camaraderie, growth, healing, and peace. As for our daycare provider, after discussing my thoughts and feelings with my wife, my concerns were alleviated, and I kept myself under the threshold of reaching an obsessive state. In the end, we found a great provider, and our daughter loves it there.

If there are issues identified during the conversation and there is a mutual understanding that it's unhealthy and/or harmful, the next step is to make modifications to one's environment and routine that avoids the issue altogether and diverts attention to more important matters. Our environment has a profound influence on our behavior and actions. As such, elements that contribute to the issues identified should be removed. As an example, if someone is trying to cut back on drinking soda, it is much easier to maintain the discipline needed to resist the urge of drinking soda when there is no soda in the house. Resisting the urge to drink it is much more difficult when the soda is staged front and center on the top shelf of the fridge. Similarly, a change in routine is needed to avoid exposure to the issue. If there is a soda machine located between one's office and the bathroom, maybe it is best to travel down a different hallway when walking to the bathroom. Both strategies rely on planning ahead and perseverance. It will feel like work, but that is because it is work. However, in time and with practice, those adjustments will pay dividends that will last your entire life.

Chapter 6 Review

Points of Emphasis:

❖ Preparedness is a state of readiness, while obsession is an idea or thought that continually preoccupies or intrudes on a person's mind.

❖ Preparedness is deliberate thought and action that has an end state, while obsession is an uncontrollable, corrosive process without end.

Perspective:

❖ People who live in war-torn countries do not obsess over self-defense, as it is the state of their world. They must take deliberate and practical steps to ensure their survival. It is difficult for those of us lucky enough not to have been born in those conditions to have the ability to understand the weight those individuals carry daily. However, their perspective provides a sense of humbleness to the conversation, as self-defense and survival are one and the same.

Call to Action:

- ☐ Reflect back on your Core Values, Safety Goals, and Life Goals. Notice the end state of each goal and the supporting tasks that enable you to reach those end states. This is your compass and guide to keep you on track.
- ☐ Refocus yourself on your Core Values, Safety Goals, and Life Goals when you feel as though you are beginning to obsess and/or have unhealthy attachments to certain elements of your self-defense strategies.
- ☐ Speak to your loved ones or a professional as needed.

End-of-Section Review

Up to this point, we have discussed why and how self-defense and personal protection plays into our lives. We have discussed fulfillment through the use of Maslow's Hierarchy of Needs, conducted an assessment of our Core Values and Safety Goals, identified strengths and limitations, reviewed the process of training program development, explored practices in the field of sports psychology, and discussed the difference between preparedness and obsession. Each task is designed to provide complete awareness of ourselves. We began the process by identifying who we presently are, establishing a vision of who we want to become, and creating a road map on how to get there. Now that we have thoroughly focused on ourselves, next, we will review factors outside of ourselves that may affect events leading up to, during, and after Safety Events.

Section Two:
External Factors

"Achieving success is like hitting a moving target. Both require accuracy, the ability to counteract external factors and adjusting the sight when necessary."

Valerie J. Lewis Coleman

Now that we have built a foundation for self-development, it's time to focus outward. External factors include any and all influences outside of ourselves that have an impact on our lives. More specifically, this includes individuals who are part of a Safety Event, influence the outcome, or provide supporting services. For the sake of clarity and brevity, this book does not identify all possible external factors in regard to personal safety. Instead, I have chosen what I believe to be the most significant and relevant factors affecting our everyday lives, as well as those that are best leveraged when external resources are needed. I use a model of an onion (Figure 3) to depict the hierarchy of external factors. In it, you can see the layering of elements that play a part in our safety. The closer the external factor is to the center of the model, the more influence or direct effect the factor has on a Safety Event. The further you get from the center, the less influence or direct effect the factor has on a Safety Event.

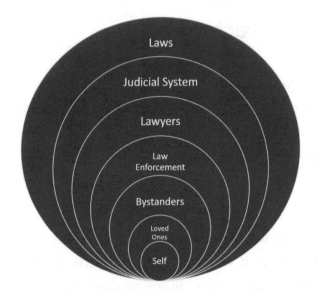

Figure 3: Onion Model of External Factors

At the center of the model is you. The first layer consists of your loved ones. The second layer is composed of bystanders present at the event. The third layer is law enforcement. Law enforcement is the last layer of the model that has an impact during the actual Safety Event. All remaining layers only have an effect before or after the event itself. So, if I wanted to get deeper into the metaphor of an onion—which I do—the first four layers are the edible portion of the onion, and the remaining layers are the peel. The edible portion provides practical usefulness. While the peel is still an important part of the onion, it only plays the role of passive facilitation.

The fourth layer is composed of lawyers and legal counselors. Lawyers are the last layer of factors that we can directly influence in real time. The fifth layer comprises the United States judicial system. The sixth layer is composed of laws and legislation pertaining to violent crime, self-defense, and personal safety.

The last factor, which I do not consider part of the actual onion but rather its own inconspicuous entity, are the criminals who perpetrate violent crimes and crimes that take advantage of the vulnerable. Each layer has set roles and responsibilities, whether innate or developed. The goal of this section is to understand the characteristics and roles of each layer outside of the self, so as to better develop strategies that utilize the best tools for the right job—since there is nothing worse than being in a life-or-death situation where you have an entire toolbox right in front of you, but do not know how to properly utilize all the tools.

Chapter 7:
Loved Ones

"Family is not an important thing. It's everything."

Michael J. Fox

L oved ones are the first layer of external factors. I use the term loved ones because it can include any and all important individuals for whom you care about. Unlike the other external factors, loved ones are unique in the fact that they are the only factors who will need protection *and* have the ability to play an active role before, during, and after the event. Generally, they have the most potential impact, as they can be educated, trained, and mentored in safety planning. Odds are, your strategy will be to protect them, rather than to employ them into the defensive mechanism of a Safety Plan. Nevertheless, no matter their role, the best way to protect them is for them to understand their capability, role, and responsibilities—even if their role is only to flee from danger and seek safety. Even fleeing to safety is a developable skill.

Your loved ones' roles during Safety Events can be dynamic but manageable. Essentially, the roles can be devised through the utilization of four category traits: capable vs. incapable and motivated vs. unmotivated. Capable vs. incapable concerns one's physical and mental ability to act during a Safety Event. Ideally, those who are capable will provide support during an event, and those who are incapable will be protected during the event. Motivated vs. unmotivated concerns one's maturity, confidence, and spiritual motivations. Those who are motivated to have an active role should be empowered to do so. Those who are unmotivated should be educated and encouraged to find perspective on the topic of self-protection to better understand the weight and consequences of unawareness. Ignorance should not be an excuse to remain unmotivated, as ignorance is perilous. Luckily, with the right developmental strategies, everyone can at least gain perspective on the importance of Safety Plans.

The four categories of traits are combined to create four distinct profile types: capable and motivated (CM), capable and unmotivated (CU), incapable and motivated (IM), and incapable and unmotivated (IU). Each profile type should not be treated as a "label" or an "identity"; rather, these labels are a method of analysis to ensure appropriate responsibilities and development are assigned relative to the associated category traits.

Capable and Motivated (CM)

CMs are those who are able to defend themselves and are motivated to do so. Typically, these individuals are above the age of puberty, have the maturity to handle high-stress situations, and do not need direct adult supervision.

Capable and Unmotivated (CU)

CUs are those who are physically and mentally able to defend themselves but are not yet at the point where they have the confidence and/or aspiration to learn how to do so. As this is the result of personality and personal perspective more than ability, individuals who fit the CU profile may lack maturity, knowledge, or worldly perspective.

Incapable and Motivated (IM)

IMs are those who are eager to be able to defend themselves and others but do not yet possess the abilities to do so. This can apply to individuals who are younger and physically immature, those with physical or mental disabilities or limitations, those who are inexperienced in technical skills, or those who lack formal training.

Incapable and Unmotivated (IU)

Lastly, those who are IUs do not have the capability to protect themselves and do not have an interest in gaining the skills to be able to do so. Therefore, they do not play an operative role during Safety Plans. IUs may consist of small children and individuals with disabilities who do not have the physical, mental, or emotional ability to protect themselves and others.

Formulating responsibilities of loved ones will be based on the current capabilities of the individual. It will be reiterated later, but all Safety Plans should prescribe responsibilities based on *current* capabilities and not potential capabilities. If an individual has not been educated and trained on how to use a defensive weapon, they should not be responsible for using it. If an individual is assigned to call the police but does not know how to use a particular phone, they should not be assigned to do so—and so on, and so forth.

In general, CMs can be integrated into any part of a Safety Plan. Ideally, they are best suited for the primary tasks of de-escalation, escape, or neutralization. IMs and CUs typically can be utilized to perform supporting tasks that are performed away from the danger or threat. This could include calling the police, looking after others in a safe location, or providing first aid. IUs are those who are dependent on others for protection, and as such they have no set responsibilities.

Figure 4 below depicts the relationship between focused traits and individual development. Development is tailored to the specific profile type in the same manner of the process outlined in Section

One, with consideration for age appropriateness. The four types of development are based on focused traits, which are physical (strength and physical ability), mental (problem-solving and intellect), emotional (maturity and maintaining composure), or spiritual (understanding of life and death), shown at the top and left tabs of the matrix. The type of development, shown on the right and bottom tabs of the matrix, is specific to the focused trait. Motivation is developed through awareness and perspective, usually through historical or current events that show the reality of the situation. Meanwhile, capability is developed through education and training specific to a skill.

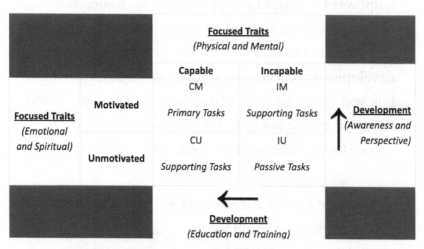

Figure 4: Developmental Matrix

Although I believe in constant development in all four focused traits, we will only focus on what is needed to move the other three profile types into the CM profile.

Capable and Motivated (CM) Development

CM development can focus on any of the four, based on strengths and limitations. The only consideration that may be needed will be based on the needs of a Safety Plan. Meaning, if there is a task or skill that is needed to successfully complete a Safety Plan but there is not currently an individual assigned to that task or skill, the development can be focused on that area to fill gaps.

Capable and Unmotivated (CU) Development

CU development should focus on emotional maturity, spiritual stability, and being informed. The goal is to empower CU types by supporting their understanding of the subject matter and why we must meet our safety and security needs. Patience will be a huge part of this development process—as you can lead a horse to water, but you can't make it drink. Remember, we are not trying to create soldiers for war; we are empowering people through knowledge, awareness, and skill.

Incapable and Motivated (IM) Development

IM development should focus on physical training and mental development. This is relatively straightforward, as they are more tangible goals: run faster, learn hand-to-hand defense, learn how to use equipment, etc. In the cases of minors or those with physical or mental disabilities, developmental focus should be on tasks that can be performed independently. The goal is to enable the individual to increase their self-sufficiency within a group, as well as provide them with a way to mitigate threats when separated from others.

Incapable and Unmotivated (IU) Development

IUs should focus on all four areas. Note: if the IU individual is a young child, the four areas of development should be aligned with life skills and general development. When implementing safety and protection training with minors and young children, it is best to emphasize avoidance, prevention, and finding a trusted adult. Lessons such as understanding "trusted adults," safely crossing the street, and not touching a hot stovetop are a great place to start.

Loved ones are by far the most important aspects of the onion model and life in general. They are both a part of my and many others' Core Values. As such, they should be a part of every consideration of every situation, including events of safety and self-defense. We have an obligation to provide safety and protection while also acting in a way that enables and empowers them to protect themselves, as we cannot be everywhere at once. This is a limitless task and should be seen as an experience of bonding, growth, and fulfillment.

Chapter 7 Review

Points of Emphasis:

❖ Loved ones are unique external factors since they are the only factors who will need protection *and* have the ability to play an active role before, during, and after the event.

❖ The four profile types for development consideration are: Capable and Motivated (CM), Capable and Unmotivated (CU), Incapable and Motivated (IM), and Incapable and Unmotivated (IU).

❖ Generally, CMs are able to perform primary tasks of a Safety Plan; IMs and CUs can perform supporting tasks of a Safety Plan; and IUs perform passive tasks or seek safe spaces during a Safety Plan.

Perspective:

❖ All development, security or otherwise, should be a bonding experience. Forcing the issue may cause resistance or resentment, perhaps both. Aligning their Core Values with the development program will increase the likelihood of interest and enjoyment.

Call to Action:

☐ Complete the Program/Curriculum Development Worksheet in the CTA Workbook for your significant other, each member of your household, and/or any loved one.

Chapter 8:
Bystanders

"The measure of a civilization is in the courage, not of its soldiers, but of its bystanders."

Jack McDevitt

The second layer of external factors is composed of bystanders. Bystanders are any individuals in the immediate vicinity of the ongoing event who are not actively a part of it. They are physically present and have the ability to affect the event through their own initiative or through your influence on them. The key to understanding bystanders is that they are basically wild cards. They can be a positive factor and provide solutions and assistance, but they can also be a negative factor and cause panic or escalation. They can also be a neutral factor by remaining indifferent, either observing from a distance, only recording the event with their phone, or ignoring the situation altogether. The difference-maker is understanding how bystanders may react, motivating capable bystanders to act, and knowing when to only rely on yourself.

We all would like to think of ourselves as people of action and champions of justice. If someone is in need, we want to help. If someone is in danger, we want to intervene. But it is not always that easy to do. Many situational factors dictate whether or not we will act in a situation in which we have little or no background information.

The murder of Kitty Genovese has become the most infamous case of the bystander effect. The murder happened in 1964 when Kitty Genovese returned home from work around three in the morning. She had been stalked by Winston Moseley, who had followed her all the way back to her apartment building. Moseley first attacked her with a hunting knife outside of the apartment building but was allegedly scared off when a man yelled from his apartment window to leave her alone. Once Moseley fled, Ms. Genovese was able to get inside her apartment building, but collapsed inside the vestibule. Approximately ten minutes later, Moseley returned, continuing his attack and subsequently leading to the rape and murder of Ms. Genovese.

Initial reports stated thirty-seven individuals witnessed the attack. This number has now been reduced to around twelve, but the fact remains that no one effectively intervened to definitively end and deter the attack. Now, I haven't performed a full-on case study myself, but many other cases do show similar trends. As such, no matter the actual number of individuals who witnessed the attack, it is taken as a fact that at least one neighbor witnessed the attack and yelled out for the attacker to leave her alone. At that moment, shouting at the attacker was an effective deterrent, as it caused the attacker to stop and flee the scene. This is a perfect example of how the smallest intervention can create real solutions.

The larger circumstance with this particular event is why no witness physically came to the aid of Ms. Genovese, even if it was just to ensure she was not hurt and to escort her back to her apartment. Now, there can be many explanations for this. They could have been too tired to walk down, thought the attack was over and that she was indeed unharmed, thought maybe it was just a dispute between a couple, or perhaps they simply did not want to get involved.

A simple internet search of "cases of bystander effect" will lead you to this case and other infamous cases like it. There are some researchers who refute the idea of the bystander effect, but some of these cases show clear tendencies in human behavior. As such, we cannot ignore them, as our safety and the safety of others might be affected by the action or inaction of our neighbors.

Truthfully, bystanders maintain the same roles and responsibilities we do as individuals. They are responsible for their own personal safety and the safety of those for whom they care. For this reason, we cannot expect them to act outside of that responsibility. They have no obligation to assist in our efforts, and we have no reasonable expectation that they will do so. Ideally, we would like to utilize bystanders as tools of intervention during an event. However, since bystanders are not vetted before an event, it is almost impossible to be able to suitably employ a bystander in a supporting role. With loved ones, we were able to place them into roles based on capability and motivation. We do not have that privilege here. Bystanders' capabilities and motivations are unknown. It is for that reason that bystanders are considered to be an unpredictable factor, as there is a possibility they can escalate an event just as much as they have the possibility of assisting in de-escalating the event.

Before we can understand how we can use bystanders, we must understand how bystanders generally act. There are two major theories that help us better understand bystanders: the bystander effect and herd mentality. The bystander effect is an occurrence where the likelihood of individuals intervening decreases as the number of people around the event increases. This is important to consider when you are in larger crowds. Some of the most common reasons why bystanders do not intervene is the belief that others will help, the belief that they will be negatively affected if they intervene, the belief that they will look stupid or abnormal to other bystanders, they do not know all the details of the situation, or they simply just do not want to get involved. The internet age has greatly influenced the bystander effect, as individuals are now more likely to pull out their phone and record an event rather than intervening. Now, this occurrence could be beneficial after the fact, as evidence for a legal case is important. However, this does little to ensure safety, counteract danger, or prevent an event from escalating.

The bystander effect can be more easily understood when viewed through the lens of herd mentality. Herd mentality is the collective mindset of groups of people. It explains the influence of the masses and how groups of individuals will act and think with the "herd." When observing certain groups of animals—flocks of birds, for instance, or schools of fish—one can clearly see that the group acts as a unit instead of separate individuals. This is similar to the phenomenon of peer pressure, where no one wants to feel like the outsider of the group, so they do things to be accepted that they wouldn't normally do (the classic examples being smoking cigarettes or drinking alcohol in high school to be "cool"). The difference, though, is that herd mentality can be reactionary rather than strictly social collaboration.

Specific to Safety Events, herd mentality could cause a group of bystanders to all act in a united front, either for the positive or the negative. A positive united front can take the form of counteracting the offender(s), assisting others in escaping, or administering first aid. A negative united front can take the form of antagonizing the offender(s), joining with the offender(s), or causing mass panic and hysteria (e.g., when protests turn into riots).

Because of this, the size of the herd is important. Consideration of bystanders are based on two main types: small crowds and large crowds, with some consideration for specific demographics such as age and cultural background. Smaller crowds—we'll say less than fifty people—have a better chance of being influenced to take action. But even then, it must be on a one-on-one basis. Singling out individuals is more likely to cause an individual to act when requested, like when you tell one specific person to call 911 during an emergency. When trying to allure others to assist you, you must be specific. Trying to speak to the group itself will only cause people to sink into the crowd. Speaking directly to people by name, or a general, "hey, you," can increase the likelihood that they will follow along.

In larger crowds—more than fifty individuals—it becomes more difficult to influence the group as a whole or the individuals within it. As such, larger groups are usually seen as an obstacle or means of concealment. I use the term obstacle when a crowd hinders the ability to move freely or reach avenues of escape. Inversely, concealment, within this setting, is the act of blending into the crowd—in the same way school of fish stick together to decrease their odds of getting singled out by a shark.

This concept does not mean you should think of others as human shields or inanimate objects. I can't emphasize that enough. Instead, this concept is meant to emphasize the strategy of positioning, which is further explained in Chapter 22. Here, positioning is specific to placing yourself in an advantageous physical position in relation to a crowd. If being proactive and cautious, it can mean positioning yourself where you always have a clear and unimpeded escape route— usually on the outside perimeter of the crowd, and ideally next to an exit or open avenue. If confined within a crowd during a Safety Event, consideration is needed based on the proximity of the threat and the potential risk of being trampled.

Consideration should also be taken when the composition of bystanders are a certain age and cultural background. Age not only dictates the ability for an individual to intervene but also dictates the dynamic of the crowd itself. Younger crowds are more likely to have an unsystematic response to an event, whereas more mature crowds have more ability to provide effective assistance. Similarly, bystanders' cultural backgrounds can increase or decrease the likelihood of them intervening. Some cultures are individualistic or reserved. Therefore, individuals of that culture are not likely to intervene. Conversely, other cultures are, by nature, collective and bold, which would increase the likelihood of intervention.

As a whole, bystanders are unpredictable and uncontrollable. There are infinite factors at play with consideration to bystanders. When numbers of bystanders increase, our ability to influence decreases. Our best bet is to influence the individuals in a crowd, but even then, we do not know their capabilities, motives, or competency. The key is to be aware of potential strategies to utilize bystanders and crowds, but only rely on known solutions you can control.

Chapter 8 Review

Points of Emphasis:

- ❖ Bystanders are the second layer that have the ability to affect a Safety Event. Unlike loved ones, they cannot be developed, and we do not have a preconceived knowledge of their capability and competency.
- ❖ The bystander effect is a theory that the more people observing an event, the less likely any one individual will intervene. Herd mentality is the theory that members of a group will follow the thoughts and actions of the group they are in.
- ❖ Increase bystander intervention through direct

engagement and tasking. Position yourself on the perimeter of crowds, as this provides freedom of movement, a better vantage point, and a decreased risk of being trampled.

Perspective:

❖ When viewing crowds, I don't see individuals; I see a unified entity. That entity is similar to a wave in the ocean—beautiful and dangerous at the same time. But viewing the group as one entity simplifies the factors in play. Individuals in the crowd only become important if they are the threat, a victim, or a resource.

Call to Action:

☐ Take note of crowds and their actions when out in public (i.e., shopping centers, sporting events, concerts, other public spaces).

  ☐ Does the crowd act as one or are there individuals sticking out from the group?

  ☐ Who is paying attention to their surroundings?

  ☐ Who is unaware of their surroundings?

☐ Begin to practice positioning in public spaces.

  ☐ Maintain pathways to exits or avenues of escape.

  ☐ Maintain clear views of the surrounding area.

Chapter 9:
Law Enforcement

"The police are the public and the public are the police; the police being only members of the public who are paid to give full time attention to duties which are incumbent on every citizen in the interests of community welfare and existence."

Robert Peel

The third layer of external factors is law enforcement (LE), due to the fact that they only affect a Safety Event once 911 has been called and they arrive on the scene. LE is the last layer able to affect a Safety Event and the only layer of external factors that have the legal authority and obligation to intervene during an event. The previous layers have the ability to intervene, but they are not protected by the same legal protections provided to LE officers. As such, LE officers are usually treated as the cure-all solution for all of society's problems. Although I do believe LE should be utilized to employ definitive solutions that can lead to prolonged safety, (i.e., arresting and the eventual prosecution of violent criminals), LE does not necessarily need to be used for trivial discrepancies that can be solved through basic problem-solving and negotiation skills. This chapter will review the official roles and responsibilities of LE, actions during and after an event, and considerations when utilizing LE in a Safety Plan.

According to the Bureau of Justice Statistics, the role of LE is to enforce laws, maintain public order, and manage public safety.[10] Take note of the exact elements of each role. To enforce laws, there must be a specific law being violated in order for LE to authoritatively intervene. Public order can be subjective, as certain laws that pertain to public order have multiple elements and thresholds, meaning it must reach a certain point before being considered a violation of a law. Managing public safety, meanwhile, covers the prevention and mitigation of circumstances that affect public safety. To put it all together, situations that require the role of an LE officer are those where a law has been violated, public order is threatened, or public safety is of concern. Specific to you and your safety, if you feel as though you or others are in danger of violence—whether it has happened or not—LE intervention should be considered. The primary responsibilities of law enforcement are investigation, apprehension, and detention of individuals suspected of criminal offenses.

---

10 "Law Enforcement," Bureau of Justice Statistics, Accessed February 16, 2023, https://bjs.ojp.gov/topics/law-enforcement.

There are three time periods of LE response that we will specifically analyze: actions during the initial call, actions at the incident, and actions after the incident. The first period is during the time LE receives the 911 call until the first officer arrives on scene. It is extremely important that you understand the time it takes for the responding officer to arrive at the scene varies based on a variety of factors and can be anywhere from minutes to half an hour. This is a lot of time for events to develop, either toward a positive outcome or negative. In other words, do not expect to make a 911 call, then be able to find the nearest recliner to take a load off. The time period of the initial call can be just as dynamic as the events leading up to and those that follow. Because of this, when you have decided to call for emergency services, you should make the call as soon as possible to allow for the upper end of the response time.

Once connected with the dispatcher, the dispatcher will follow a script and take down pertinent information in order to dispatch the correct resources. Dispatchers have usually been trained to keep the individual calm while also instructing the caller on how to mitigate any external risks during the call that could be affecting the caller. The phone call should be maintained until the first officer arrives at the scene. Internal to the department, the dispatcher's role is to provide the responding officer with critical information such as location, your phone number, general situation, information on potential victims, information on potential offenders, and current threat at the scene. This is the responding officer's first impression of the situation and will affect the officer's overall demeanor, course of action, and thought process.

It is important to provide the dispatcher with key information to warrant the best possible response from the responding officer. Key information would be your location, the nature of the threat, location of threat, and possible victims. Your location is the information that should be provided first, in case the call is dropped. This way, the responding officer at least knows where to go. There are technologies and methods of retrieving a caller's location from the phone being used; however, technology does fail, and certain methods can take time. You can't rely on other systems, especially when you are able to provide the information yourself. If you don't know the exact address, describe the distance and direction from a known address, even if it's just, "I'm two blocks from the McDonald's on Main Street."

Explaining the nature of the threat provides the responding officer with the information needed to formulate a course of action and initial posture. If the threat is described to be imminent, like with a home invader currently in the house, the officer knows to advance to the threat quickly with high awareness. If the threat is described to be present but mitigated, either by distance, obstacles, or by force, the officer knows they have the ability to access the scene before taking any decisive action. Location of individuals on scene provides the responding officer a mental map of what to expect. This is important, as they evaluate where they should place themselves at the scene when they arrive, just as we position ourselves based on the location of the attacker(s) and bystanders. It is also important for target discrimination. The easier the responding officer can distinguish between victims, bystanders, and any offender, the better.

The second period is from the time that officers arrived on the scene to the time that they have success-fully defused the event. During this time, we will analyze LE's general course of action as well as the potential positive and negative outcomes. Knowing what they do and how they do it will help you plan ahead for when they arrive. Courses of action include, but are not limited to, mitigation, crisis intervention, arrest, or lethal force. It is possible that if no crime has been committed, or the victim of a crime does not want to press charges, the officer will primarily act as a mitigator. This is often seen in domestic calls where there has been a verbal confrontation that has not escalated to the point of physical assault. Usually, the officer acts to defuse the situation through de-escalation techniques and recom-mending one or all parties leave the area.

Crisis intervention is similar in that the officer is there to resolve the crisis through verbal intervention;

however, crisis situations involve individuals who need the help of medical professionals, so the intervention and de-escalation techniques are specific to the type of ailment. Similar are cases when an individual is having a psychiatric episode or may be under the influence of drugs or alcohol.

Arrest is the primary course of action taken by LE when a crime has been committed and/or the victim would like to press charges. This is pretty straightforward, but the event leading up to an arrest can be dynamic and range from verbal or physical altercations, foot chases, car chases, and everything in between. Lastly, LE may need to use lethal force when there is imminent threat of life to the officer(s) or others. However, the level and type of justification vary by jurisdiction.

From these courses of action, I created a matrix (Figure 5) for consideration pertaining to LE involvement. The matrix is not a deterrent to dissuade you from calling the LE, but rather, it can be used when considering and mitigating certain factors once LE arrives on scene. The matrix is based on direct vs. indirect and wanted vs. unwanted effects.

Possible Outcomes from LE Involvement		
	Wanted	**Unwanted**
Direct	• Protection • Event Resolution	• Possible Escalation • Limited Ability to Affect Situation once LE Arrive
Indirect	• Increased Number of Bystanders and Witnesses • Police Report	• Lasting Effects Between Individuals Involved

Figure 5: Matrix of Possible Outcomes from LE Involvement

Direct wanted effects are considered to be the on-site protection and the definitive resolution of the Safety Event. When LE is on scene, they are trained to control the affected area and the personnel within it. This should lead to a safer, controlled environment. Eventually, the controlled environment leads to the definitive resolution of the event. This is ultimately the biggest benefit of LE, as civilians do not have legal authority to pursue certain strategies to resolve an incident, namely the forced physical removal of a threat.

Indirect wanted effects are considered to be an increase in bystanders and a paper trail that can be used for legal action. Nosey neighbors and curious passersby are going to want to know what's going on if LE are present. Although they will not be able to be in close proximity, as it might impede the officers' duties, those individuals could be potential witnesses if and when the attacker is charged with a crime. Additionally, a police report may hold valuable pieces of information that weren't evident during the event. For instance, the police report will contain information from various perspectives, which may provide insight into the event beyond your own perspective. When compared to and pieced together with your account of the event, you will have a more complete picture that will serve as the basis for future prevention and protection strategies.

Direct unwanted effects include times when their presence will actually escalate the situation and the overall loss of control of the individuals involved. Once LE arrives on scene, they legally control the area. This means all actions, including those of the caller and victims, are the responsibility of the present officers. As such, once LE assumes command over the situation and affected area, their presence and/or actions may lead to an escalation. The worst-case scenario here would be the use of lethal force.

Here, the consideration is whether the situation falls under the responsibility of LE. Verbal altercations are an example where LE intervention may not be the best course of action. If a dispute has presented no threat of harm or the violation of a law, LE intervention could have adverse effects. The cases I'm mostly referring to in this example are those where the parties involved are in a disagreement and LE is called to act as a mitigator and quasi-therapist. Note: verbal threats, acts of intimidation, and unwanted physical contact do fall under situations where LE intervention is warranted.

Indirect unwanted effects can have potentially lasting effects between the parties involved. Depending on the threat or relationship between parties, LE involvement could cause intensification of a threat. Now that definitive action has been taken against a particular party, the individual(s) may look to get even, regain some sense of reputation or control, or fall deeper into their delusions. Note: this is not to dissuade a decision to utilize LE, but rather a recommendation to think beyond LE intervention by preparing for long-term, sustainable protection and prevention of future incidents.

Lastly, we will consider the third time period: the actions after the event. This is from the time the threat or event has been successfully resolved to the time all LE leave the scene. During this time, LE may gather additional information for the police report, secure the area for evidence collection, and/or provide and allocate resources for victim care. In regard to the individuals affected by the event, this will be a drastic shift, as they will be going from a state of high stress into a state of reflection and deliberation. As such, it may be difficult to regain composure in that amount of time to be able to provide valuable information to the LE on scene.

Don't feel pressure to give a statement or answer questions if you are unable to completely regain normal composure. Take physical, mental, and emotional care of yourself and your loved ones first, and assist law enforcement at a later time, even if you need to go to the department to give your statement there. But do not neglect to give a statement, since the report itself can be beneficial. This report can be used to initiate further investigations or be used by the victim as evidence of an ongoing situation when pursuing legal action. If children are involved, it is best if they are interviewed by a forensic interviewer, as they have specific training with children. But once again, only if they are in a good place physically, mentally, and emotionally. Additionally, the LE on the scene may have information on how to contact victim advocates. Victim advocates can assist you in connecting with needed services as well as help you along any legal processes that may follow.

Law enforcement officers play a vital role in maintaining order and safety in any society. They can be a resource before, during, and after a Safety Event and have the official authority to act in ways that an ordinary citizen cannot. As with any external factor, there are a variety of variables that may need to be considered, such as their unfamiliarity of the event details when responding and their authority to use a range of force. To ensure their service is optimal and aligns with your needs, be certain you are providing accurate and timely information while maintaining security measures until the event has been resolved.

Chapter 9 Review

Points of Emphasis:

❖ LE's role is to enforce laws, maintain public order, and manage public safety. LE is the last layer of external factors that have an effect during a Safety Event.

❖ When providing information to the dispatcher, the most important information to provide is location and phone number, nature of the threat, and location of the threat and victims.

❖ When LE arrives on scene, they will act to neutralize active threats and control the surrounding area.

❖ Once the incident has been resolved, LE will take information from involved parties and witnesses to complete their report on the incident. This report can be used to initiate further investigations or be used as evidence of an ongoing situation when pursuing legal action.

Perspective:

❖ LE deals with the dissolute side of society all day, every day. That type of wear and tear can change their demeanor, mindset, and even outlook on the job. As with any profession, there are employees who are extraordinary at their jobs and others who should pursue other endeavors. LE is no different. No matter the type of LE you may interact with, you can help them help you through your competency and preparedness.

Call to Action:

☐ Visit your local police department's website to get an idea of the department's focus, initiatives, and culture. If interested and available, sign up for their newsletter to stay informed.

☐ Meet and speak with law enforcement officers in your area. If interested, set up a ride-along to get a more in-depth insight on what their job entails on a daily basis.

Chapter 10:
Lawyers

"The leading rule for the lawyer, as for the man of every calling, is diligence."

Abraham Lincoln

The fourth layer of a Safety Event's external factors is composed of lawyers. This layer is the start of factors that play a systemic role in the United States judicial system. As you will see, the judicial system does not play an active role during an event, but it is a factor that can aid in prevention and post-event undertakings.

Lawyers are part of every aspect of the judicial system, but in regard to the subject matter of this book, lawyers may assist you in civil action against individuals who pose a threat to your well-being, ensure your Safety Plans and methodology abide by all pertinent laws, and can defend you in a court of law in cases where you are charged with a crime due to acts of self-defense. Though there are stigmas and opinions about lawyers, the truth is they can provide valuable services and assistance. Lawyers are not all one and the same—they must be properly vetted to ensure they are the right fit for you. Additionally, the law is vast, and lawyers tend to specialize in one or a few areas. For these reasons, I will go over the criteria of what to look for when finding a lawyer, so they align with your Core Values and understand your Safety Goals and legal needs.

The role of lawyers is to act as a legal agent on behalf of individuals, organizations, and government entities in legal proceedings. Their responsibilities include, but are not limited to, studying laws, rulings, and regulations; conducting legal research and gathering evidence; explaining law, procedures, and policies; providing legal advice to clients; preparing pleadings, notices, and making appearances in court; and representing clients in legal proceedings on civil or criminal matters. Essentially, lawyers are the liaison between you and the legal system. You can even look at them as interpreters, with the goal of ensuring you understand the court and the court understands you. Lawyers are held to a high ethical and legal standard and therefore must always perform their duties through ethical and legal practices. We will only analyze their role in prevention and post-event, as they do not have an active role during an event.

Hiring a lawyer is analogous to hiring an employee. When hiring an employee, you are hiring an agent that will represent a company. When hiring a lawyer, you are hiring an agent that will represent you. As such, the process is similar. You will want to do some initial searches to find a pool of potential lawyers, ask for referrals from people you trust, conduct a background check, and conduct a consultation interview. General internet searches will provide you a list of lawyers, but I recommend using the websites Avvo and Martindale. These sites will provide you client and peer ratings, as well as many filters that will narrow down your search based on your needs. Asking for referrals from family, friends, and others is also a good way to find trusted lawyers—or hear about ones to avoid. I always like getting firsthand accounts from people I trust, as their experience provides reputable evidence.

Once you have a list of around three lawyers you think may be a good match for you and your needs, you should conduct a background check on them. Contact your state's bar association to confirm they are in good standing and review any past or pending inquiries into ethical violations. Any confirmed ethical violations are a no-go for me, as a lawyer's entire reputation is based on their knowledge and practice of the law and their ethical conduct. Not only that, but they have an incredible amount of power over their clients' well-being, money, and even freedom.

Lastly, when you finally have a list of potential lawyers who look to be a good fit, are in good standing with the state bar association, and have no ethical violations, you can reach out directly to their law office to schedule an initial consultation. Most law firms provide a free initial consultation up to a certain amount of time, usually thirty minutes to an hour at most. During the consultation, the lawyer will ask for a general review of the case. It is important to tell the whole story in chronological order, including all the facts—especially the facts that may hurt your case. After hearing your story, they should be able to tell you their general thoughts on the case, expected time frame and associated costs for their work, and if they are able to represent you.

Some lawyers will not be able to take the case due to conflict of interest or decide not to take it based on personal choice. If the lawyer states they can represent you, be sure to put the terms of payment and scope of work in a written agreement (your lawyer should be prepared to create this type of written agreement, typically called a "retainer agreement" or similar). Verbal contracts can be legally binding, but it's best to have a document you can refer to that details the scope of practice and terms of financial compensation when needed. Before you officially hire a lawyer, they will not be able to go into detail about your specific case or provide you legal advice. This is to protect both of you. Once hired, you and your lawyer will be able to talk freely with confidentiality.

A lawyer can be useful for understanding your legal rights, risks, and limitations, advising you on the best courses of action in legal matters, and serving as an overall resource for understanding the legal system and applicable laws. Lawyers should, first and foremost, be used as a legal resource to ensure you are within your legal limits. I recommend speaking to a lawyer once you have reviewed pertinent local, state, and federal laws. That way, you have a basic understanding so your lawyer can fill in gaps, correct misunderstandings, or elaborate. We will review some of the more common laws pertaining to self-defense in an upcoming chapter. Each state, and the jurisdictions within them, maintains its own set of laws, so it is crucial you review the laws where you reside.

Another place where lawyers are useful is in situations that involve ongoing conflict and threat of harm, such as instances of domestic violence, stalking, ongoing harassment, and so on. Here, lawyers can advise and make recommendations on how to mitigate the conflict or threat and explain potential legal courses of action. The aim is to utilize an additional resource that parallels other efforts in preventing conflict and offering protection from harm. It is possible the legal advice given is not the most advantageous strategy when dealing with a given conflict or threat—for example, because it could possibly escalate a situation or provide a false sense of security. Remember, the lawyer is only concerned with legal proceedings, which is only one aspect of the entire situation. Ultimately, you are the only person who understands the entire situation and its implications, so it is your decision if and when the legal strategy will be used.

The roles and responsibilities of the lawyer post-event are where the lawyer makes their money, figuratively and literally. In addition to being a strategic planner and resource, the lawyer will be your representative and advocate before the judicial system. At the time a Safety Event occurs, it is recommended to consult your lawyer only after an event has been completely resolved and all parties have been cared for mentally, physically, and emotionally. The well-being of those involved is first and foremost the top priority post-event. Once aftercare is provided for those who need it, consulting a lawyer as soon as possible is the next priority, as there is a chance that as time elapses, details of the occurrence will start to blur or be swayed by afterthoughts. If feasible, consulting your lawyer can happen concurrently while caring for the well-being of those involved. I only stress caution, since it is easy to get tunnel vision by wanting to make sure those responsible are held accountable for their actions.

It is beneficial to consult your lawyer as soon as possible, as they will only then be able to begin working on the case. Getting your lawyer involved will free up your intellectual and emotional capacity, thereby allowing you to proceed with your normal life quickly. Generally, the lawyer will ask you for your narrative of the event, supporting evidence such as records, documents, or photos, and then follow up with specific questions that will narrow the legal strategy most effective for your case. Once a lawyer has all pertinent information and explains to you the overall strategy, they will assume responsibility for the case. Essentially, this means they will be performing most, if not all, of the legwork. They will conduct research, prepare and file paperwork, and consult you when further information is needed or to update you on the case. They may plead your case in writing, through filings at the courthouse or letters to other parties, and/or orally, through negotiations and arguments during court, by advocating for the law to be applied to the facts of your case to reach the best outcome for you. There may be times when you need to be present with your lawyer (such as in interviews, depositions, or court appearances), but many times, they will be working on your behalf without your continual presence. For this reason, it is important you understand exactly what course of action is being taken, how it affects you, what you are expected to provide, and the possible outcomes of the case, both favorable and unfavorable.

Remember, lawyers represent you—meaning they act on your behalf, not on their own accord. Furthermore, there is immense trust placed with a lawyer, since a case's outcome is heavily affected by the lawyer's competent representation rather than just the overall narrative of "right" vs. "wrong." Be selective about who you hire. Choose the lawyer that fits your case, strategy, and values. Do not be afraid to speak up when you are unsure or do not like the direction the strategy is taking. Stay informed and ask questions so you understand exactly what is being done in regard to the joint effort between you and your lawyer and with your case as a whole. If the lawyer ends up not being the fit you initially thought, you can terminate the relationship and continue the case with a different lawyer.

Overall, a lawyer provides a vital service, as it is unrealistic that we are able to take on the same roles and responsibilities they would while still trying to maintain our normal job, family obligations, and life.

Chapter 10 Review

Points of Emphasis:

❖ Lawyers act as legal agents and your representative and advocate before the judicial system.

❖ Lawyers are useful for educating you on legal policies and procedures, conducting legal administrative tasks, and setting legal strategy.

❖ You are still responsible for your own well-being. Do not blindly rely on the lawyer to "solve" your problems for you. Work with and through the lawyer to align legal options with your overall Safety Goals.

Perspective:

❖ Lawyers are intelligent, analytical thinkers who may or may not have the appropriate interpersonal skills. Due to the nature of the profession, they are very methodical about how they act and convey points of conversation. Much of this is to ensure they are maintaining the ethical standards set forth by their state's bar association. However, there is a clear difference between being helpful and being harmful.

Call to Action:

☐ Conduct a preliminary search on lawyers in your area using www.avvo.com and www.martindale. com.

☐ Narrow down to three lawyers based on scope and price.

☐ If and when needed, conduct an initial consultation with the three identified lawyers to review your needs and scope of work.

☐ If and when needed, choose and hire the lawyer that fits your Core Values, needs, and budget.

Chapter 11:
The US Court System

"Laws are a dead letter without courts to expound and define their true meaning and operation."

Alexander Hamilton

The fifth layer in our onion of external factors is the judicial system. Outside looking in, the US court system may seem complicated and hard to understand. This is partially true, as the court system and its processes can be convoluted. Of course, its complex design is due to delicate subject matters, as it is vital to the court's legitimacy to ensure due process and set procedures. It's important to understand how our court system is set up so that, when pursuing legal action, you have a more streamlined understanding of the administrative and judicial processes. We will cover the general structure of the judicial system, the general processes of the judicial system, legal actions that can be taken, and specific strategies pertaining to those actions.

The purpose of the judicial system is to provide a fair process for parties to present their grievances with equal justice under the law—emphasis on "fair process," since we know it's not always a "fair outcome." Within the judicial system, the roles and responsibilities of the judges are to interpret law and to arbitrate and adjudicate conflicts between parties. The court system is a structured hierarchy, meaning each court system is designed for a specific jurisdiction. The higher the jurisdiction, the more influence on the entire state—or even the entire country.

The federal court system, which focuses on US federal laws (that is, laws enshrined in the US Constitution or enacted by the US Congress), is generally composed of District Courts, Courts of Appeals, and the US Supreme Court. The lowest level, District Courts, are trial courts, where evidence is heard, facts are decided, and verdicts are rendered. This is what you probably think about when you envision "court." The intermediate level is the Court of Appeals, which handles appeals of US District Court cases. Courts of Appeals do not hold trials or find facts, but rather decide whether US District Courts committed errors in interpreting or applying the law. The highest level of the judicial system is the US Supreme Court, which chooses at its discretion which cases it will hear—typically only cases of high importance or controversy when it comes to the interpretation of the US Constitution, federal laws, or disputes between states.

State and local court structures are set up by state legislatures and constitutions, and their titling and structures can vary widely. However, the relationship generally remains the same between the levels of hierarchy, with the lower "trial courts" that find facts, apply the law, and render verdicts; "appeals courts" that hear appeals arguing that trial courts committed legal errors; and a top-level "supreme court" (though in some states, it has a different name) that is the final arbiter on cases that are highly important or controversial regarding how state laws or state constitutions are interpreted. The relevance to this book is to understand the procedures of trial courts as well as appellate court decisions, and their effects on you as a US citizen. Understanding court procedures can better prepare you in the event that you find yourself involved in legal proceedings, as only figuring it out while going through the process will result in unnecessary growing pains and stress.

Legal action can be achieved through civil lawsuits or criminal lawsuits, sometimes both for the same matter. Civil lawsuits can be initiated by individuals or organizations against individuals, organizations, or government entities. They are used to determine whether a particular party is liable for wrongdoing, damage, or injury to another person or entity, and if so, to determine the appropriate remedy (usually monetary compensation). Criminal lawsuits, on the other hand, are initiated by violation of a law(s) and may only be pursued against an individual(s) or organization(s) by local, state, or federal governments. Self-defense as a concept and how it is applied in both criminal and civil cases will be explored in the following.

Civil Lawsuits

There are various types of civil cases. Here, we are concerned with protection orders (also known as restraining orders) and civil lawsuits involving bodily harm or the threat of bodily harm. Both types of civil matters are initiated with the filing of a petition. A petition is a formal written request to a court to issue an order using the rule of law. The person filing the petition is known as the petitioner, while the respondent is the person responding to the petition. In self-defense cases, the respondent is the individual being accused of assault, harassment, communicating threats, etc. After service of the petition, a hearing date is established, and the respondent has the opportunity to contest the matter. Depending on the jurisdiction, emergency temporary protection orders may be an option when the matter cannot wait until the assigned date of the hearing. At a protection order hearing, a judge will hear the case and make a ruling either to enact a protective order or deny it. In a civil lawsuit, the petitioner and respondent will appear in front of the court for numerous hearings over a period of time to litigate and resolve the matter. If it does not resolve, the matter will go to trial, which may be held before a judge or a jury.

In civil matters, the burden of proof is on the petitioner, and the allegations must be proved by a preponderance of the evidence. "Preponderance of evidence" means that it is *more likely than not* that a particular claim is true. Therefore, the petitioner needs only provide enough evidence to demonstrate that it is more likely than not that the respondent committed an alleged act or is a current threat to the petitioner's safety.

Protection orders are enacted with the intent to prevent harm and are issued when a petitioner can demonstrate that the respondent has caused harm in the past and is likely to cause future harm to the petitioner. Among other restrictions, protective orders have the ability to prohibit the respondent from any form of communication with the petitioner, coming within a certain distance of the petitioner, maintaining possession of any weapons, or going to the petitioner's home, work, or school.

Once a judge grants a protection order, any violation of that order may lead to a warrant for the respondent's arrest, and criminal charges for the violation may be filed. Charges for violation of a protective order serve to protect the petitioner, especially where past offenses did not result in charges being filed, charges were filed and later dropped, or the trier of fact found the offender not guilty.

It is important to note that a protective order is just that: an order. It does not provide tangible protection to the petitioner, who is generally a victim of violence. Because protective orders are civil matters, the respondent is not held in custody, and thus remains free. It is not uncommon for individuals who have protection orders issued against them to see the order as simply a piece of paper; those who take that view do not typically comply with the orders of restriction. There is also the possibility that the protective order may escalate the situation by further feeding the offender's delusions or anger. It is important to weigh the risks versus the benefits when pursuing a protective order, as it is not a definitive solution. Instead, it should be seen as a legal option that parallels other security and safety strategies.

Criminal Lawsuits

Understanding criminal lawsuits is beneficial whether you are the victim of a crime, witness to a crime, or are unfortunate enough to find yourself as the defendant. For serious criminal violations, a criminal lawsuit begins with a court or grand jury issuing an indictment, which is a formal accusation that a person or organization has committed a crime. To obtain the indictment, a govern-ment-employed lawyer commonly called the "prose-cutor" formally files a claim with the court on behalf of the People/State against the defendant and presents evidence that the accused has committed a crime. If the court or grand jury determines that the case has merit (at this stage, the court's or jury's job is not to decide whether the accused is guilty or innocent, and there is typically no need for a defense case or counter-argument), it is allowed to proceed, and the indictment is issued. A warrant for the defendant's arrest is then issued and carried out by law enforcement. If the crime is less serious in nature, the defendant may instead receive a citation requiring them to appear in court. The defendant is then arraigned, and the case is litigated between the district attorney's office and a criminal defense attorney. A good majority of criminal cases resolve in guilty pleas and don't go to trial. At a trial, the defendant has the option of having a trial by judge or a trial by jury, both of whom are considered to be the triers of fact. The trier of fact determines after the presentation of evidence and arguments whether the defendant is guilty or not guilty.

In criminal cases, the prosecutor bears the burden of proof to prove beyond a reasonable doubt that the alleged offense(s) was committed by the defendant. The burden of proof in criminal cases is much larger compared to those in civil cases. In a criminal trial, the victim is the State or the People's lead witness and must generally testify against the defendant at the trial. In practice, the prosecution will dictate the trial strategy, although there are other ways to help ensure a solid case against the defendant.

In a trial, the prosecution is required to present evidence to the trier of fact to prove its case, which may come in various forms. Although evidence is generally thought to be—and indeed is—collected by law enforcement and experts, it is highly recommended to document as much as possible. That may include writing down details of the crime, maintaining records of conversations, or taking photographs or videos before, during, and after the offense.

As you can see, processes and actions directed by the courts are not completely flawless solutions. While legal processes may aid in protection, the responsibility for an individual's complete safety falls on our shoulders. Protection orders may assist in prohibiting unwanted behaviors or serve to give rise to criminal charges if the restricted party violates the order. But they can also antagonize the respondent and cause escalation that may lead to further violence. Criminal charges against a defendant may lead to incarceration, which will provide physical protection, but only for the amount of time that the individual is incarcerated. Security and protective measures should be planned for and implemented if there is a chance of release and the risk of physical or bodily harm persists.

The information listed in this chapter is merely an overview of the court system and its processes. As a takeaway, it is important to understand the general administrative processes of civil and criminal courts, what protective orders are and how they can be used to ensure a victim's safety, and how to document accounts of the offense so it can be used in a trial to support your and/or the victim's claims. The court system alone cannot be depended upon to provide complete security and protection; although it is a process that does protect victims, there are still those who find themselves in situations of violence again. The court system is administrative by nature and moves at a relatively slow pace. As such, unless the offender is incarcerated, other security measures should be actively employed while judicial processes are ongoing to ensure the safety of those at risk.

Chapter 11 Review

Points of Emphasis:

❖ The judicial system is meant to provide a forum for parties to present their grievances and apply the law to resolve legal disputes.

❖ Civil lawsuits are used to hold a particular party liable for wrongdoing, damage, or injury.

This includes protection orders, which are civil lawsuits that prohibit contact from individuals who are accused of violence, threat of violence, or harassment.

❖ Criminal lawsuits are formal allegations of a violation of US law against an individual(s) or organization(s), and they are pursued by local, state, and federal governments. Criminal lawsuits are retroactive and are used to hold individuals accountable for their transgressions. They can provide definitive protection when the sentence is incarceration.

Perspective:

❖ Think of the court system as a means to an end: a means to ensure those who wish to do harm to others are separated from the general public—and you. However, until an individual is incarcerated, they will still be a threat. And if their sentence does not include life without the possibility of parole, they may be a threat in the future.

Call to Action:

☐ Go to your local courthouse, or the courthouse's website, to gather information on
   ☐ filing a petition for a protection order
   ☐ filing a criminal complaint
   ☐ resources for victims of violent crime

Chapter 12:
US Law

"What is the most sacred duty and the greatest source of our security in a Republic? An inviolable respect for the Constitution and Laws."

Alexander Hamilton

In the United States, there are several sources of law: constitutions (basic and generally unchanging rules and rights for governance of the people), statutes (passed, amended, and repealed by legislatures), administrative laws (rules put in place by government agencies), and common laws (decisions by judges, often also called "case laws"). The law makes up the last layer in the onion model, since we as individuals have little direct influence over the legislative process (other than electing legislative officials), but laws do have a direct effect on us. It is important to know and understand laws, as they are your limits as a citizen. Breaking them, due to ignorance or not, leads to the same consequences: fines, restitution, parole, or incarceration.

The purpose of this section is to provide you a foundation to begin identifying and understanding laws that are relevant to your personal safety and self-defense. You should know your constitutional rights, laws specifically pertaining to self-defense, as well as laws that are meant to deter people from harming others. This section will begin from the top with constitutional law, then work down through federal, state, and case law. Considering the extensiveness of the topic, we will only review what is generally important and relevant.

As the saying goes, "I'd rather be judged by twelve than carried by six." For those of you who don't know, this is a popular phrase meaning one would rather do what is necessary to defend their life, even using deadly force and risk being put on trial, than to be dead and have six individuals carry their coffin. I agree with the rationale, as being alive to defend yourself in court is far more preferable to being deceased. However, sometimes that phrase is interpreted as encouraging a rebellious mentality, or as an excuse to ignore certain laws. To neglect and ignore the law creates unnecessary risk. The most effective practical method of protecting yourself is by aligning your Safety Plans with pertinent laws. Consider that the best-case scenario is that you are alive, with no chance of prosecution, because you were lawful and justifiable in your actions.

Constitutional Law

Constitutional law refers to the rules of conduct and practices thereof that govern the relationship between sovereign people and their government. Constitutions are intentionally broad, as opposed to more specific statutes or administrative rules, but are intended to embody all best practices on how a society should run and govern itself. The US Constitution is of course the legal document establishing the fundamental structure of the United States government, but each US state also has its own constitution, setting up the rules of governance for that state. However, the US (federal) Constitution is considered the supreme law of the land, and no other law may contradict it. As so, it is important to understand the US Constitution and the place of constitutional law, since it establishes the foundation for many principles of personal freedoms, safety, and protection we Americans are entitled to. The main text of the US Constitution is devoted to creating rules about the creation, structure, and maintenance of the federal government. However, I have listed the Bill of Rights below, which are the first ten amendments of the US Constitution that purposefully bestow upon the citizens of the US undeniable rights for the purpose of safety, protection, and pursuit of happiness. Each amendment is an individual right of all US citizens, where no government body or power can deny them without due process of law.

Bill Of Rights[11]

Amendment I: Congress shall make no law respecting an establishment of religion, or prohibiting the free exercise thereof; or abridging the freedom of speech, or of the press; or the right of the people peaceably to assemble, and to petition the government for a redress of grievances.

Amendment II: A well-regulated militia, being necessary to the security of a free state, the right of the people to keep and bear arms, shall not be infringed.

Amendment III: No soldier shall, in time of peace be quartered in any house, without the consent of the owner, nor in time of war, but in a manner to be prescribed by law.

Amendment IV: The right of the people to be secure in their persons, houses, papers, and effects, against unreasonable searches and seizures, shall not be violated, and no warrants shall issue, but upon probable cause, supported by oath or affirmation, and particularly describing the place to be searched, and the persons or things to be seized.

---

11 Engrossed Bill of Rights, September 25, 1789; General Records of the United States Government; Record Group 11; National Archives.

Amendment V: No person shall be held to answer for a capital, or otherwise infamous crime, unless on a presentment or indictment of a grand jury, except in cases arising in the land or naval forces, or in the militia, when in actual service in time of war or public danger; nor shall any person be subject for the same offense to be twice put in jeopardy of life or limb; nor shall be compelled in any criminal case to be a witness against himself, nor be deprived of life, liberty, or property, without due process of law; nor shall private property be taken for public use, without just compensation.

Amendment VI: In all criminal prosecutions, the accused shall enjoy the right to a speedy and public trial, by an impartial jury of the state and district wherein the crime shall have been committed, which district shall have been previously ascertained by law, and to be informed of the nature and cause of the accusation; to be confronted with the witnesses against him; to have compulsory process for obtaining witnesses in his favor, and to have the assistance of counsel for his defense.

Amendment VII: In suits at common law, where the value in controversy shall exceed twenty dollars, the right of trial by jury shall be preserved, and no fact tried by a jury, shall be otherwise reexamined in any court of the United States, than according to the rules of the common law.

Amendment VIII: Excessive bail shall not be required, nor excessive fines imposed, nor cruel and unusual punishments inflicted.

Amendment IX: The enumeration in the Constitution, of certain rights, shall not be construed to deny or disparage others retained by the people.

Amendment X: The powers not delegated to the United States by the Constitution, nor prohibited by it to the states, are reserved to the states respectively, or to the people.

Due to the Bill of Rights, you have freedom of speech, a right to keep and bear arms, protection against unreasonable searches and seizure, the right to due process of law, the right to a speedy and public trial by an impartial jury, and protection against cruel and unusual punishment. As you can see, the Bill of Rights does not specifically speak of protection from violence or other related matters. However, as this book is written more in regard to personal protection from physical harm caused by individuals of delinquent nature, protection from unlawful acts committed by agents of official government bodies are just as important, if not more so. As much as I trust in our systems created by our Constitutional Republic, I know human nature itself is not perfect. Therefore, those who govern official governmental systems or work within them have just as much ability to cause harm, intentional or otherwise, as others whose actions disrupt the norms of society. It is for this reason that it is so vitally important to know and understand your rights as a citizen of the United States of America.

Federal Law

Federal Law is the body of law created and enforced by the federal government. Federal law retains jurisdiction for crimes that are committed in violation of federal law, or for crimes committed across multiple states. Oftentimes, violating federal law results in more severe penalties than violating state law.

There are federal laws that address weapons and apply to self-defense concepts. Individuals who choose to carry weapons as part of their Safety Plans should carry legally and lawfully. The National Firearms Act (NFA) defines the following firearms as regulatory firearms: machine guns, short barrel rifles (SBR), short barrel shotguns (SBS), suppressors, and explosives. If not purchased, carried, and employed legally, individuals are subject to a Class D felony that can result in up to ten years in prison, three years of probation, and $250,000 in fines.

State Law

State law is the body of law created and enforced by individual states. State laws vary, and it is important for individuals to know and understand the state laws applicable to them. It is also important for travelers to learn the state laws of the state they travel to, as the laws there apply to them during their stay. The first, and arguably most important, concept to understand is the parameters in which a state law permits self-defense. For the person defending themself, the actions must reach a level of justification determined by the state to be considered self-defense.

Self-defense, or defense of others, is typically justified when there is reasonable fear of imminent threat, and the response is proportional to the threat. Imminent threat means that there is physical danger, that the danger is real, that it will occur with immediacy, and may result in serious bodily harm or death. A person pointing a gun at another person is an example of imminent threat of serious bodily harm or death. A person who uses self-defense is held to what is called the reasonable person standard. The reasonable person standard, as it pertains to self-defense, requires that the actor reasonably believed that they were in imminent danger of serious bodily harm or death, and that a reasonable person would have believed the same. A reasonable person is described as a fictional person with the ordinary degree of reason, prudence, care, foresight, or intelligence, whose conduct, conclusion, or expectation in relation to a particular circumstance or fact is used as an objective standard by which to determine liability. Similar to our "average" person in Chapter 3, a reasonable person is a person with enough competence to think through a problem set and formulate a rational conclusion.

Lastly, there must be the use of proportionate force. For self-defense to be permissible, force used by the actor must be proportional in relation to the posed imminent threat. Force that is considered proportional is force that matches the level of, or is equal to, the imminent threat. For example, someone who has a loaded gun pointed at them may respond with deadly force, as the loaded gun aimed in their direction threatens loss of life. Conversely, the use of deadly force in response to being punched may not reach the level of proportionate force, unless there is justification that the punching caused threat to life.

Two opposing concepts that are important to know regarding self-defense in a public space are the duty to retreat and "stand your ground" laws. Some states impose upon an individual the duty to retreat—that is, the duty to flee from the threat of harm—before defending oneself with force, generally in a public space. "Stand your ground" laws, on the other hand, do not have the requirement that a person must attempt to flee before using proportionate force in a public area. It is extremely important for a person to learn which of the two laws their home state utilizes in order to defend oneself in accordance with the law to avoid prosecution and its consequences.

The "castle doctrine" is a legal doctrine applied to private spaces, like the home, that allows a person to use force to protect the inhabitants of a residence from an imminent threat of serious bodily harm or death. The castle doctrine is not a law in and of itself; it is a principle used by states to create laws relating to self-defense. In some states, the castle doctrine applies to private property other than the home, such as a vehicle or a person's place of business.

Each individual state has its own laws pertaining to the purchase, ownership, carry, and employment of weapons. The laws apply to different weapons in different states but generally include firearms, knives, and pepper spray. Beyond weapon ownership and employment, it is important to understand your state's laws pertaining to self-defense to understand your permissions and limits that will ultimately dictate the strategy you plan for and utilize. Not knowing, or not following, pertinent laws risks civil liability, criminal charges, and legal sanction.

Case Law

Case law, otherwise known as common law, is law based on outcomes of past judicial rulings, legally known as a precedent. Case law is unique in the fact that when precedent is set within a specific jurisdiction, it must then be followed by all courts that fall within the same jurisdiction within the same hierarchical level and lower. Moreover, case law may be considered outside of a specific jurisdiction or from a lower court, which is legally referred to as persuasive authority. Persuasive authority describes a source of law that carries some authoritative weight, but that does not bind a court to follow that law. Meaning, the previous ruling can be used to bolster an argument, but the judge does not have to follow the precedent.

Listed below are relevant cases that pertain to self-defense. All but one details cases involving the use of firearms. This is possibly due to the high-profile statuses that Second Amendment cases receive. Hence, they are heard by the Supreme Court. Nonetheless, the emphasis here is the interpretation by the court and its implication. A detailed account of each case would be far too much for the scope of this book, so I will only provide the BLUF—the bottom line, up front.

People v. La Voie[12]

In *People v. La Voie,* the court held that in the case of self-defense, an individual's subjective fear must also be objectively reasonable. By its very nature, fear is subjective. However, in a legal setting, the fear must meet the reasonable person standard discussed in this chapter.

District of Columbia v. Heller[13]

District of Columbia v. Heller is a self-defense case that set precedent on the interpretation and protection of the Second Amendment of the US Constitution. There, the court ruled that the Second Amendment protects the right to keep and bear arms, even where the exercise of that right is unconnected to military service.

McDonald v. City of Chicago[14]

Following the ruling of *District of Columbia v. Heller,* a lawsuit was filed against the City of Chicago, where the plaintiff argued that the Second Amendment applied to all states for self-defense purposes. The court ruled that the Bill of Rights apply with full force and protection to the federal government and to the states.

---

12 *People v. La Voie,* 155 Colo. 551, 395 P.2d 1001 (1964).

13 *District of Columbia v. Heller,* 554 U.S. 570 (2008).

14 *McDonald v. City of Chicago,* 561 U.S. 742 (2010).

N.Y. State Rifle & Pistol Association v. Bruen[15]

Prior to *N.Y. State Rifle & Pistol Association v. Bruen*, the State of New York made it a crime to possess a firearm without a license. Firearms could not be carried without a license, either inside or outside of the home. If an individual wanted to carry a firearm outside of the home, they could apply to obtain an unrestricted license to have and carry a concealed pistol or revolver if—and only if—the applicant could prove that proper cause existed for doing so. An applicant satisfied the proper cause requirement only where they could demonstrate a specific need for self-protection. The court ruled that New York's proper cause requirement was unconstitutional and violated the Fourteenth Amendment by preventing law-abiding citizens with ordinary self-defense needs from exercising their Second Amendment right to keep and bear arms in public.

As you can see, the very laws that determine the nuances of our Safety Plan are constantly in flux. It's important to stay informed and maintain an understanding of laws that affect elements of our Safety Goals and Plans. That way, they are always formulated to benefit from the law instead of risking our own prosecution. In other words, aligning Safety Plans with existing laws is the most efficient and effective manner to reach Safety and Life Goals, just as the other layers are best utilized when they align to your specific needs.

---

15 *N.Y. State Pistol & Rifle Association v. Bruen*, 142 S. Ct. 2111 (2022).

Layer by layer, we peeled, cut into, and diced through the entire onion, and not one tear was shed.

Chapter 12 Review

Points of Emphasis:

- ❖ Laws are a body of rules of conduct that have a binding legal force and effect and are prescribed, recognized, and enforced by a controlling authority.
- ❖ The primary sources of law are constitutions, statutes, regulations, and case law.
- ❖ Self-defense or defense of others is generally justified when there is reasonable fear of imminent threat and the force used is proportional to the threat presented.
- ❖ Depending on your state, you will need to abide by duty to retreat or stand your ground. Duty to retreat requires the threatened individual to attempt to flee the threat of harm before proportionate force can be used, generally in a public setting. Stand your ground, on the other hand, does not require an individual in a public space to attempt to retreat before utilizing force that is proportionate to the threat.
- ❖ If adopted by your state, the castle doctrine is a legal doctrine that allows a person to use force to protect the inhabitants of the home.

Perspective:

❖ Ignorance is not justification for breaking a law. No matter if you know of or understand a law in the jurisdiction you reside in, if you violate a law, you can be tried and punished for the offense(s). Protect yourself by educating yourself.

Call to Action:

☐ Complete the Legal Worksheet in the CTA Workbook.

Chapter 13:
Criminals

"If violent crime is to be curbed, it is only the intended victim who can do it. The felon does not fear the police, and he fears neither judge nor jury. Therefore what he must be taught to fear is his victim."

Lt. Col. Jeff Cooper

B ut why is all this consideration needed? What is truly the underlying problem? And why did I just spend six chapters learning about a made-up metaphorical vegetable of analytical exhaustion? Well...because of humans that can cause so much pain and suffering that the very life you now know would be turned into a yearning memory. (My apologies for being a Debbie Downer.)

More accurately, a "criminal" is a person who has committed a crime. However, here I am speaking in a broader sense of someone who has caused, or has had intent to cause, physical, mental, or emotional harm to others. "Transgressor" would probably be a more accurate term, as it is defined as a person "violating law or command or going beyond a boundary or limit."[16] However, for the sake of simplicity, I will use the term criminal, as the research used in this book is based specifically on criminal activity and the real act of breaking laws.

This chapter will cover general profiling, methodology, psyche, and trends of criminals. This topic is deep and expansive, so I can only provide general, high-level information. However, the goal is to get a sense of who the individuals are who would take advantage of other people, what they do, how they act, and why they do it, so we are better prepared to counteract their wrongdoings.

To know our adversary, we must first understand them. The teachings of Sun Tzu in *The Art of War* explains that to avoid defeat, we must know ourselves and our enemy.[17] Luckily, we have already done half of that in Section One. Now, all we need to do is understand the enemy. (Dun dun duuuuuuun) Our "enemy" is considered to be the potential person(s) who would inflict harm on ourselves and our loved ones. Knowing your enemy is arguably the single most valuable piece of knowledge one can utilize in a self-defense

16 "Transgressor Definition & Meaning," Dictionary.com, Accessed March 15, 2022, https://www.dictionary.com/browse/transgressor.

17 Stephen F. Kaufman, *Art of War: The Definitive Interpretation of Sun Tzu's Classic Book of Strategy* (New York: Tuttle Publishing, 2012), 31, https://search-ebscohost-com.ezproxy.umgc.edu/login.aspx?direct=true&db=nlebk&AN=1567300&site=eds-live&scope=site.

scenario—or any scenario, for that matter. Athletic teams utilize this concept to gain an athletic advantage over opposing teams. Businesses utilize this concept to gain a competitive advantage over competing businesses. And the military uses it to gain battlefield advantage against military foes. It is possible to create a favorable outcome without having intimate knowledge of an enemy, although it does create more of a challenge and relies more on luck than strategy. Plus, it is an unnecessary impairment since information is so easily available and abundant.

When preparing for both of my deployments, I made sure to do as much research on the enemy as possible. Not only did I want to know and understand their military tactics, capabilities, and vulnerabilities, I wanted to understand their culture, their way of thinking, and ultimately why they were who they were. In a sense, it is empathy, as it is possible that if our situations were swapped and I was born into their life, I could be the same as they are—maybe even worse. Understanding their ways is not designed to provide them an alibi or an excuse for harming others; it is a means of protection. Ideally, this is done through a mental and emotional state free of discrimination, bias, and hatred. Knowledge cannot exist in a state of emotional unrest, as our opinions will skew and modify "facts" to fit our motives and objectives. I understand this is not always easy, especially for those who have already been victimized, but it is necessary—not only to counteract those who wish harm on others, but for ourselves, as there is no peace without understanding.

Understanding the "why" before the "who" makes it a bit easier to see the complete picture. Motives and impulses bridge the gap between intangible character traits and tangible action. This is similar to how we established Core Values to establish goals, ultimately leading to implementing a plan of action. One's Core Values, vis-à-vis their character traits, set the tone for their motivations and actions. Even a criminal has Core Values that drive and direct their actions and goals. There are many theories meant to explain the cause and effect of violent behavior, but here, we are only concerned with the link between the two based on the clarity it provides. Also note we are only concerned with violent crime, abuse, and exploitation. Regardless of the crime, the main motives of criminal behavior are power and control; obtaining status, whether financial or as a part of a group; physiological impulses, such as survival or sexual in nature; and mental health disorders.

Power and control refer to the drive of gaining and maintaining power and/or control of oneself or over another individual(s). This can be seen from two perspectives. There are those who act to gain control, whether perceived or real, over themselves. Conversely, there are those who act to keep others in their control or desire a sense of power over systems or people.

Obtaining social status is similar, as it can be a form of power among people but does not necessarily need a direct element of power or control. Status can be in the form of finances, status within a group, or connection.

Physiological impulses cover sustainable needs and sexual desires. Lack of sustainable needs may cause a survival response, which leads to acting self-interestedly without consideration of others, such as stealing money when you can't afford food.

Sexual desires may cause individuals to act to fulfill sexual fantasies or satisfy a sexual urge.

Mental disorders, outside of antisocial personality disorders, cause dysfunction in the brain due to physical or chemical abnormalities. Mental disorders cause a distortion in perception where the individual does not perceive the world or their actions the same as the average individual.

I do not lump in antisocial personality disorder, otherwise known as sociopathy, with mental disorders since there has not been a clear link established between biological development and the behavior. Those who have antisocial personality disorder, otherwise known as sociopaths, are the first and major personality type we will discuss. According to the Mayo Clinic, sociopaths show the following repeated signs and symptoms:[18]

---

18 "Antisocial Personality Disorder," Mayo Clinic, February 24, 2023, https://www.mayoclinic.org/diseases-conditions/antisocial-personality-disorder/symptoms-causes/syc-20353928.

- Ignoring right and wrong.
- Telling lies to take advantage of others.
- Not being sensitive to or respectful of others.
- Using charm or wit to manipulate others for personal gain or pleasure.
- Having a sense of superiority and being extremely opinionated.
- Having problems with the law, including criminal behavior.
- Being hostile, aggressive, violent or threatening to others.
- Feeling no guilt about harming others.
- Doing dangerous things with no regard for the safety of self or others.
- Being irresponsible and failing to fulfill work or financial responsibilities.

That is quite a laundry list. Sociopaths create general cause for concern since their behavior traits show tendencies of harming others. Not only that, but usually their efforts are persistent, extensive, and diverse. Furthermore, the fact that they are usually perceived as charming and intelligent makes it difficult to associate them with the crimes they have committed. Being able to recognize these signs in others will provide insight into who to keep a closer eye on, who to distance yourself from, and who to protect yourself from. That is not to say that having one or two of these traits makes you a sociopath, as I'm sure we all fall under at least two on the list. However, the more traits an individual exhibits, the more precaution should be exercised.

Beyond sociopaths, other personality traits of criminals include entitlement, rationalization, perceived invincibility, sentimentality, lack of purposeful ambition, and impulsiveness.

Entitlement is described as always requiring personal benefit. It is a severe version of selfishness, as usually, selfishness refers to only thinking of oneself. Entitlement believes that they are owed something out of every interaction.

Rationalization is the ability to create excuses for their behavior. This is a type of loophole for the criminal, which provides them the ability to harm others and have no remorse. By creating justification, or a reason behind their action, they then do not feel the need to feel bad about their actions, because there was *obviously* a very good reason for it to occur. Even when the reason seems outrageous to a sensible person, it is seen as logical and reasonable by the criminal. This is seen with cult leaders, who justify exploiting others because they were "helping" their victims.

Perceived invincibility is the belief that they cannot be captured, found out, or killed. Essentially, it is a bloated ego that causes a false sense of optimism.

Sentimentality is the connection one has to an idea, object, person, or group. The severe form of sentimentality is obsession, where all the traits we covered before are present. Stalkers are a good example, as eventually, their unhealthy sentiment consumes them past the point of reason.

Lack of purposeful ambition is the state of living without purpose or perseverance. Individuals who lack financial, social, and educational support will be tempted to commit crimes to fulfill certain needs, since it is seen as the easier alternative. In a sense, they are taking the path of least resistance. It is easier to burglarize an unlocked vehicle than it is to maintain a nine-to-five, full-time job.

Lastly, impulsiveness is the inability to make sound, rational decisions and the tendency to instead act solely based on an emotional state. The emotional state could be hatred, sadness, excitement, or fear.

Considering different crimes require different methodologies, each crime requires specific consideration when analyzing. However, there is one common trend: criminals prefer the "easy target." Just as a predator prefers an easy kill for its food, criminals would rather not have to work too hard for their reward. As such, they seek out individuals they believe to be vulnerable or less able to counteract them—individuals who travel alone, females, those under the age of eighteen or older than sixty-five, those who are not paying attention to their surroundings, etc. By victimizing vulnerable individuals, criminals increase the likelihood of accomplishing their objective without getting caught by law enforcement with little risk of harm to themselves.

Crime Area Study

Conducting an Area Study of your surroundings will provide you with the specific information needed to ensure your plans and strategy address the issues, crime, and threats that are most likely to occur. Generally, an Area Study is multidisciplinary research of a specific geographical location. They can get really in-depth and really detailed, really quickly. Our purpose is to gather enough information to achieve an understanding of what crime to look out for and what to do about it. Generally, the information needed is found on the websites of your local police and sheriff departments, usually depicted in a crime map. State and federal agencies provide crime data as well, but considering that those data sets are statewide or nationwide, the information is generally too broad to be useful, unless you are developing strategies for mass shootings, acts of terrorism, human trafficking, etc. In those cases, you should research best practices provided by research organizations and federal agencies. But since being a criminal analyst is not our full-time job, we will only skim the surface of the Five Ws: who, what, when, where, and why.

Who

The "who" focuses on general traits and characteristics of criminals as a whole, although they can also be specific to individuals. Key details to know are age, gender, identifying marks such as tattoos, style of clothing, and behavioral traits. Knowing "who" isn't meant to create a target. It is meant for awareness, as identifying characteristic patterns early on can increase chances of avoidance and prevention.

What

The "what" focuses on the criminal act and methodology. Key details to know are what crime is being committed; whether or not weapons are used; type of engagement such as coercion, force, or surprise; and maneuvering tactics of how they target and pursue the victim. The "what" provides awareness as well as specific actions and resources needed to counteract.

When

The "when" focuses on the date and time these crimes are occurring. Key details to know are how frequently crimes occur, time of year, seasonal occurrence, which days of the week, and what time of day. The "when" provides information for avoidance.

Where

The "where" focuses on the physical locations in which the crimes occur. Key details to know are the general location, such as the neighborhood, shopping centers, street, etc.; whether it was residential or in public space; whether it was in a populated area or underutilized area; and whether it is expanding into other areas. The "where" provides information for avoidance.

Why

The "why" revisits the type of crime being committed with additional analysis. The purpose is to understand the motive so as to better enact a plan of action or follow-up plan in case an event happens. For instance, if vehicles are being broken into for money and valuables, but you also figure out identification is being taken, it's likely the thieves are using or selling personally identifiable information that can then be used to steal your identity. Therefore, victims of these crimes would need to take steps to ensure their identity and accountable resources are protected.

Knowing is half the battle. By gaining insight on who criminals are, what they do, when and where they do it, and why, we are able to narrow down our efforts to mitigate the risks we are more likely to encounter. Additionally, we can formulate effective countermeasures to specific criminal efforts and methodology, which grants us the ability to neutralize the threat while mitigating risk of harm. Generally, criminal behavior and characteristics can follow trends we identified. But there is variability, as there is with all things. Conducting an Area Study helps narrow the scope down to what is most relevant. Learning best practices from research organizations and governmental agencies ensures comprehensive knowledge and preparedness for all threats. If we put in a little time up front and do the research, we can understand criminals better than they understand themselves, and counteract them entirely.

Chapter 13 Review

Points of Emphasis:

- ❖ Understanding criminal behavior, methodology, and tactics provides specific insight that can guide the direction of preparedness, avoidance, and counteraction.
- ❖ The main motives of criminal behavior are power and control; obtaining status, whether financial or as a part of a group; physiological impulses, such as survival or sexual in nature; and mental health disorders.
- ❖ Some common personality traits of criminals include entitlement, rationalization, invincibility, sentimentality, lack of purposeful ambition, and impulsiveness.
- ❖ Area Studies can be used to gain a general understanding of the types of crime and methodology in your local area.

Perspective:

❖ We like to perceive criminals, or those who harm others, as something other than human. In truth, there is a certain percentage that have the ability for rehabilitation. However, another percentage will continue their transgressions for as long as there are people for them to victimize. There is a place and time to help others, but not when you or your loved ones are in threat of harm.

Call to Action:

☐ Conduct an Area Study by completing the Area Study Worksheet in the CTA Workbook.

☐ Conduct research, using the corresponding websites, for best practices when preventing and counteracting instances of:

   ☐ Rape/Sexual Assault: nsvrs.org
   ☐ Mass Shootings: dhs.gov
   ☐ Kidnapping: missingkids.org
   ☐ Domestic Violence: thehotline.org
   ☐ Stalking: stalkingawareness.org

End-of-Section Review

In this section, we reviewed relative external factors through a model similar to that of layers of an onion. At the center of the onion is you. Starting at the center of the onion working outward, each layer has its own effect on you as an individual while you have the ability to affect each layer in some way, shape, or form. By understanding each layer's effect, and possible resources related to that layer, you can formulate comprehensive strategies when facing immediate and ongoing threats. Loved ones need protection while also having the ability to assist during Safety Plans. Bystanders have the ability to directly affect a Safety Event in real time, but the effect and outcome will vary. Law enforcement officers are official agents with granted authorities beyond the scope of an ordinary citizen. Lawyers act as legal liaisons between the bigger judicial system and you as a citizen. The judicial system acts as a system of legal bodies and processes that can provide retroactive means of accountability for wrongdoing. Laws either grant or limit authority for you as a citizen when acting to protect yourself and others. And lastly, criminals and those who act to maliciously harm others are the reasons the onion is so important to understand. Their actions cause systematic and detrimental effects that require the utilization of all available resources to ensure the personal safety of you and your loved ones. Specific to your strategies, each layer should be analyzed for its general effect, its factors that support your strategies, and those factors that cause deviations and adjustments.

Section Three:
Prevention and Preparedness

"An ounce of prevention is worth a pound of cure."

Benjamin Franklin

Prevention is the single most important aspect of safety, self-protection, and self-defense. If the event never happens, or you are not present during an event, there is no risk of harm to you or your loved ones. The concept of preventive medicine, or medical care that prevents and mitigates disease processes before they become too problematic, demonstrates that it is easier and simpler to maintain a healthy lifestyle rather than needing medical intervention to treat a condition. The same is true here. Although unexciting and perhaps mundane, risk prevention goes a long way in sustaining the overall well-being of you and your loved ones. In this section, we will learn how to examine risks, formulate Safety Plans and Standard Operating Procedures, and conduct various types of rehearsals—all of which will provide an optimal level of preparedness and, with it, a peace of mind.

Chapter 14:
Understanding Risk

"Disaster mitigation...increases the self-reliance of people who are at risk—in other words, it is empowering."

Ian Davis

Risk is around us every minute and every second of every day. We take risks when we get in our cars to drive to work, risking an automobile accident. We take risks when traveling up and down stairs, risking tripping and falling. We also take a risk by choosing not to act, because of fear or lack of confidence, risking the loss of opportunities for fulfillment and development. Risk is inevitable, but fortunately, risk is mitigable. We can control how much risk we have in our daily lives. The only problem is that risk is subjective, so it may be difficult to know what to prioritize. The goal is to mitigate the risk that has the most chance of occurring or has the most severe consequences. This is why it's important to know how to identify relevant risks and how to conduct a Risk Analysis. Here, a Risk

Analysis includes identifying a known or potential threat, assessing the risk level of the threat, and prioritizing mitigation planning and strategy based on risk level and relevance.

Identifying risks isn't inherently difficult. However, the goal is to identify the risks that are relevant to you, your loved ones, and your goals. We do this by referring back to your Core Values. Your Core Values will be your baseline when identifying risks, since these are the most important entities in your life and any risk to them should be taken seriously. And obviously, your personal safety and the safety of your loved ones will be the main examples used in this section, as they are often exactly what is at risk during a Safety Event.

Simply put, the way to identify risks is to ask yourself this simple, yet tangled question: "Who goes where, and does what, around who and/or what?" This question helps us identify the person or thing we are trying to keep safe from the person or thing that could cause harm, in a particular environment.

The easiest way to do this is by listing those individuals you wish to protect—your loved ones— and then writing out their schedules. Their schedule will provide the established times and locations for consideration. Next, you will identify who or what will be around them, or has the likelihood of being around them, at each location at that particular time. For example, little Jimmy during the school year will travel from home to the bus stop around 7:00 a.m., rides the bus to school from 7:15 to 8:00 a.m., is picked up by Mom at school at 3:00 p.m., goes to the park from 3:15 p.m. to 4:00 p.m., and arrives home around 4:30 p.m. So, the places that needed to be analyzed are home, the route to the bus stop, the bus stop itself, the bus, the school, the car ride with Mom, and the park.

At this point, we have answered the first part of the question. Now we just need to answer the last element of who or what could potentially threaten little Jimmy's well-being in those places. This task can be facilitated by a Risk Tree Analysis. The Risk Tree Analysis (RTA) is similar to a Decision Tree Analysis, which is used to display possible scenarios based on potential choices. Essentially, it is a tool to help businesses and individuals in their decision-making process. Here, we have modified it to display possible risks based on our daily schedule and potential choices. RTAs can begin at any point in time for any scenario, but for the sake of continuity, we will continue with the example above and begin with the start of little Jimmy's day. Figure 6 shows the RTA diagram of a segment of little Jimmy's schedule. While Figure 7 shows a more simplified version that includes the entire daily schedule.

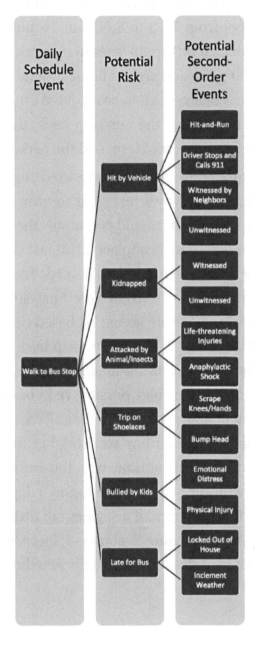

Figure 6: Risk Tree Analysis Diagram Example

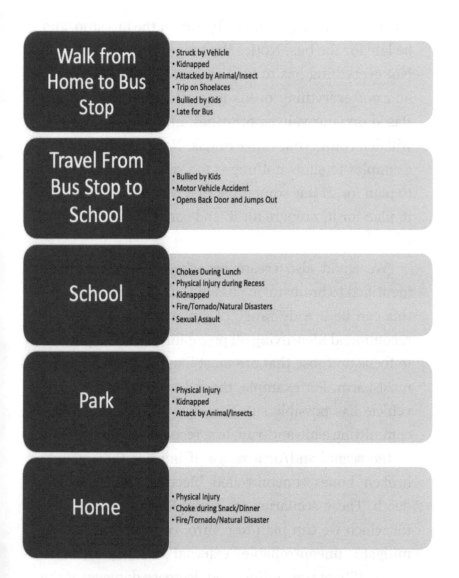

Figure 7: Simple Risk Tree Analysis Diagram Example

Referring back to Figure 6, little Jimmy starts his day by going to the bus stop. We have identified potential risks for this action above. little Jimmy could: be hit by a vehicle, get kidnapped, get attacked by an animal, trip on his shoelaces, get bullied by kids at the bus stop, and be late for the bus. Notice the range of risks identified. Not everything has to be a scenario of life and death, and not everything needs to be thoroughly analyzed. Based on your values, priorities, and perspective, you will determine your range of risk. Note: I am providing examples to show nothing is too severe or too "crazy" to plan for. If it is something that worries you, identify it, plan for it, prepare for it, and continue on with your life.

We could also create branches from those risks identified to brainstorm possible sub-scenarios. Again, this can be a wide range of scenarios, so although I recommend identifying all possibilities, it is important to focus on those that are most likely or will cause the most harm. For example, the risk of being struck by a vehicle has possible sub-scenarios such as the driver committing a hit-and-run, first responders being called to the scene, and/or a range of injuries that include broken bones, uncontrolled bleeding, and possibly death. These scenarios are examples of contingencies for which we can plan to control controllable factors, mitigate uncontrollable external factors, increase probability of prevention, and decrease damages if the event occurs.

Referring back to some of the research you have already done on the particular situation will assist you in focusing on the most relevant, more severe, and higher probability outcomes. Little Jimmy tripping on his shoelaces is not worth a significant amount of time of planning, since the chances of that happening are relatively small with only minor consequences. With this being said, the next tool we will use will weigh the possible risks in order to identify the ones that do need in-depth analysis, those that need greater consideration, and those that can be disregarded until new data suggests otherwise. This process is done by using a Risk Matrix.

A Risk Matrix, shown below in Figure 8, is a tool that visually displays the level of risk by showing the relationship between the probability of occurrence and its consequences. The Risk Matrix does a good job of prioritizing and putting theoretical risks into perspective, but there still is some thinking involved. The probability of occurrence can be an educated guess, but empirical data would help increase its accuracy. Or, perhaps, the probability of occurrence will be based on individual traits and tendencies. It could be deemed more likely (60 percent to 89 percent) someone who is considered clumsy will trip and fall, whereas an Olympic gymnast's probability of tripping is unlikely (< 10 percent). Consequences and their severity are more straightforward, as cause and effect is an easier concept to predict. Tripping and falling on a flat carpet surface may only rise to the level of minor severity. However, when tripping down a flight of stairs, the severity rises to the level of major, as, depending on the height, the fall could cause broken bones or a head injury.

		Probability Of Occurrence				
		Practically Impossible /Unlikely ≤ 10% (1)	Less Likely 10% – 39% (2)	Likely 40% - 59% (3)	More Likely 60% - 89% (4)	Certain/ Has Occurred ≥ 90% (5)
Severity of Consequence	Not Significant (1)	Low (1)	Low (2)	Low (3)	Medium (4)	Medium (5)
	Minor (2)	Low (2)	Low (4)	Medium (6)	Medium (8)	High (10)
	Moderate (3)	Low (3)	Medium (6)	Medium (9)	High (12)	Very High (15)
	Major (4)	Low (4)	Medium (8)	High (12)	Very High (16)	Very High (20)
	Severe (5)	Medium (5)	High (10)	Very High (15)	Very High (20)	Very High (25)

Figure 8: Risk Matrix

Probability of occurrence is rated from practically impossible/unlikely to certain/has occurred. This makes it easier to make a rough guesstimate, but if you are more number-minded, you can measure probability by numerical percentages. Severity of consequences is categorized by the range of not significant to severe. Not significant would be the equivalent of an injury sustained from a cuddly puppy attack, while severe usually means loss of life, limbs, or eyesight. The heart of the matrix (the colored squares in the center) shows the risk level. This is categorized as low, medium, high, and very high. The number in the parentheses is a way to assign numerical value to each category, which creates an overall score for the risk. The higher the score, the more severe the risk. One is the lowest value for a possible risk, while twenty-five is the highest value for a possible risk.

In general, low risks need less consideration and the least amount of mitigation strategy, while very high risks should be generally avoided. Ideally, medium and high risks should be planned for and mitigated until they can be classified as low risk. This means the mitigating strategies decrease the likelihood of the event occurring while also decreasing the severity of the consequence and increasing the preparedness to deal with those consequences. It's important to note severe consequences start out with a medium risk level. This is due to the fact that if there is even a slight chance of loss of life, limbs, or eyesight, interrelated factors must be prevented or mitigated. A common example of this is wearing a seat belt in a motor vehicle, as motor vehicle accidents can lead to loss of life, limbs, or eyesight.

Continuing with the example, I'll use the Risk Matrix to identify the level of risk from both being hit by a vehicle and tripping on shoelaces. As stated previously, my educated guess on the probability of tripping on shoelaces by any particular kid would be 20 percent or less likely (this might be a modest guess, for some of you parents out there). I would also theorize that the most severe consequence would be minor, perhaps a scrape on the knee or hand. Looking at the matrix, that would put the risk level at low (4/25). On the other hand, the probability of a pedestrian getting struck by a vehicle is less than 1 percent, based on the total occurrences within the US.[19] With less than a 1 percent chance of happening, it is considered unlikely, but since the possible consequences are severe, this would put the risk level of being hit by a car at medium (5/25). Note: I went with the nonspecific probability (the 1 percent probability) for simplicity's sake. Just like our Area Study, the probability is based on factors specific to the situation and environment. For example, if it is a common occurrence for drivers to speed or drive recklessly in a specific residential neighborhood, the probability should be considered higher than the general 1 percent. Always consider all possible factors during risk assessment.

Life is full of risks, whether physical, emotional, or spiritual. Most are mitigated through general lifestyle habits and do not pose a significant threat. The key is to be able to identify those that do pose a significant threat and require consideration and planning. Using the Risk Tree Analysis and Risk Matrix provides valuable

---

19 "Pedestrian Safety," Centers for Disease Control and Prevention, May 13, 2022, https://www.cdc.gov/transportationsafety/pedestrian_safety/index.html#:~:text=You%20can%20take%20steps%20to%20keep%20yourself%20safe,a%20sidewalk%20or%20path%20instead%20of%20the%20road.

tools to do just that. The process itself ensures you are thinking of all possible outcomes and risks while assigning quantitative value to an otherwise subjective subject matter. Generally, risk assessments only need to be completed once for any one particular scenario—i.e., going to and from school, outings to shopping malls, attending a concert, etc.—and then reevaluated if there is a major change in people, places, or environmental factors. Once the more relevant and severe risks have been identified, you are now able to develop a Safety Plan designed to mitigate those same risks.

Chapter 14 Review

Points of Emphasis:

❖ Risk is diverse, widespread, and ever-present. Ignoring it does not mean it doesn't exist. Understanding and mitigating risk is fundamental to any aspect of survival.

❖ Conducting a Risk Analysis includes identifying a known or potential threat, assessing the risk level of the threat, and prioritizing mitigation planning and strategy based on risk level and relevance

❖ The process of identifying risks can be simplified by focusing on our Core Values and/or the most important aspects of our lives and discerning potential dangers that may affect them.

❖ Risk Tree Analysis (RTA) is a process of identifying threat contingencies and potentially dangerous scenarios that may arise during a specific event in time.

❖ A Risk Matrix is a tool that visually displays the level of risk by the probability of occurrence and its consequences. The Risk Matrix prioritizes and puts intangible risks into perspective through the relationship between the likelihood of occurrence and severity of consequence.

Perspective:

❖ We all conduct risk mitigation every second of every day, whether we are crossing the street, driving, taking a hot dish out of the stove, or the classic running with scissors. We have gained a certain understanding of everyday risk so we know why it must be mitigated and how to do so. Self-defense follows the same practice but with a bit more deliberate consideration.

Call to Action:

☐ Complete the Risk Analysis Worksheet in the CTA Workbook and perform a Risk Analysis for situations relevant to your and/or your loved ones' daily schedule.

Chapter 15:
Safety Plans

"Let our advance worrying become advance thinking and planning."

Winston Churchill

Safety Plans are where your personal skills and development become the tools for practical solutions. Sometimes used interchangeably, Safety Plans and Courses of Action (COA) are definitive solutions to Safety Events. There are two sayings that sum up the importance and dynamics of planning: "Failure to plan is planning to fail," and "Everyone has a plan until the bullets start flying." Although they might seem contradictory, both statements are true. Not having a plan creates too many unmitigated circumstances, and any factor unmitigated can cause force-multiplying effects. On the other hand, some plans change instantly when a life-or-death incident occurs. As you will see later, this is not necessarily a bad thing, if you have a backup plan. Adapting to overcome negative circumstances is just as important as having a plan to begin with. The preparation process we will follow ensures that even when a plan changes based on certain circumstances, you will have plans B, C, and so on ready to employ. The two-step process we will follow to ensure comprehensive mitigation and successful navigation of a Safety Event consists of 1) COA development and 2) contingency planning.

The military has the rule of 20/80, which dictates that before a mission, planning should only take up 20 percent of the total preparation time and rehearsals should comprise the other 80 percent. This rule is designed to prevent leadership from spending too much time planning—as they *looooove* planning. It is also designed so all soldiers involved in the mission have enough time to conduct rehearsals of the planned actions to ensure a seamless and mistake-free execution. I bring this rule up to provide perspective. Although planning is important, *really* important, it should not comprise the majority of your time. In fact, the actual COA development process should only take one to two hours. With practice and experience, the process will only get faster.

Step 1: COA Development

COA development is exactly what it sounds like: developing a list of prioritized actions to implement when confronted by a threat. In general, COA development is used to develop major movements to achieve our Safety Goals during a Safety Event.

Types of COAs

For our purposes, the four main COAs are: avoidance, escape, neutralization, and delay and resist, usually in that order. This order of COAs allows for quick adaptation to any Safety Event when needed.

Avoidance

The number one goal in most Safety Plans should be avoidance. The concept is pretty straightforward—if you are not located where the danger is, the danger poses no threat. Of course, this only applies to situations where information was available beforehand, such as severe weather, planned riots, infamously dangerous locations, cases where cautionary signs are posted near hazardous locations, etc. The keys to avoidance are awareness and information. In this day and age, information is readily available, so it is somewhat easy to gather relevant information through a general internet search or to keep up with current events. This is also where your Area Studies prove their worth. Once your Area Studies are completed, you will have a good feel for what areas, places, or types of activity to avoid.

Escape

When avoidance is not an option, escaping is considered to be the next best COA. Escape is creating enough time and space between you and the offender where the offender is no longer an immediate or near-immediate threat. This is a bit subjective, as the space between and the classification of immediate and near-immediate is based on the contributing factors. An attacker carrying a knife while standing in front of an individual is immediate, but when a locked door separates them, the threat becomes near-immediate. Near-immediate could also be when the threat is in the same building three floors above. Or, in the case of horror movies, near-immediate means the threat is a full mile away on foot. Yet, when you pull your vehicle over to call 911 at the nearest gas station, there they are waiting for you. To put it simply, escaping is achieved when completely outside the range of danger. When in doubt, continue moving to increase the distance and time between you and the threat.

Neutralization

The next preferable COA is neutralization. Since not all scenarios will allow for an escape as a possible solution, neutralizing the offender is the next best option. I use the term neutralize to convey the overall goal of rendering the offender harmless. This can be done through de-escalation, containment, restraint, or—in the case of high-risk situations—lethal force. De-escalation is the act of reducing the active threat by means of verbal resolution. Containment is the act of hindering one's freedom of movement through means of structural confinement (i.e., enclosed in a room, building, or structure). Restraint is the act of hindering one's ability to move through means of physical or mechanical control (i.e., zip ties, handcuffs, or pinning to the ground). Lethal force is any means of force that has the ability to inflict severe injury that may cause death.

Ideally, these methods of neutralization are used through the process of escalation of force. Escalation of force is a concept commonly used in law enforcement and military referring to the policy of using nonviolent, to least violent, to most violent means of dealing with a threat. When used conceptually, our order of neutralization methods are de-escalation, containment, restraint, then lethal force. However, not all scenarios will provide you the ability to try each one before moving on to the next. So, it is important to react according to your capability and current situational factors.

Delay and Resist

The last and least desirable COA is delay and resist (D and R). D and R is less of a deliberate COA and more or less enacted by default. Meaning other COAs, such as escape or neutralization, have been implemented but have not been successful. As such, D and R is essentially buying time until you are able to escape, neutralize the threat, or a third party intervenes. This can be accomplished through verbal negotiation, physical maneuvering by maintaining a safe distance, or a combination of verbal and physical strategies depending on the disposition of the threat. More than likely, the third party will be law enforcement, but it could be any third party that has the ability to successfully end the event. Think prisoner of war (POW) trapped behind enemy lines. The mindset is to stay vigilant and continue to make a conscious effort so that when an opportunity arises to enact a more preferable COA, you are in a position to do so. There's often no way of knowing how much time is needed and how safely it can be bought. However, if your back is to a wall and there are no other options, it's better to maintain a fighting chance than to give up.

COA Principles

COAs should be formed based on the five principles of simplicity, timeliness, flexibility, redundancy, and realism. This not only ensures effectiveness when executed but also provides subjective measures that can then be used to compare proposed COAs. Considering you may formulate multiple COAs for one scenario, weighing them against each other ensures the best-suited COA is chosen. You may also choose to pick elements of different COAs to combine into one super-duper, secret-weapon, megazord (*Power Rangers* reference) COA. As long as they abide by the following principles, your COAs will help you in these Safety Events.

Simplicity

As with all things, the simplest solutions are the best solutions—it is no different here. Simple COAs ensure that everyone who is a part of the plan and event knows what should happen and what will happen, as is the case with school fire drills. The siren goes off, the children stand up, form a line, and follow the teacher outside. Creating a plan with too many steps or complicated processes will increase the chances of confusion and mistakes. Confusion and mistakes increase risk of harm.

Timeliness

The principle of timeliness mirrors that of simplicity, as the quickest plan mitigates confusion and decreases the chances of other external factors arising. "Speed is security" is practically the mantra of small unit tactics, and it is no different here. When moving quickly and efficiently, you may find yourself out of danger as fast as you were brought into it.

Flexibility

The principle of flexibility considers the realization that you cannot realistically plan for every factor, nor is every plan executed to perfection. Remember the saying, "Everyone has a plan until the bullets start flying"? This is a portion of why that statement is so true and why we develop plans A through Z. Well, maybe not through Z, but certainly, at the very least, having a plan B. Flexibility dictates that some elements of a plan will be more of a parameter rather than relying on a single specific detail. These parameters will be based on established Standard Operating Procedures and more specifically PACE plans, which are covered in detail in the next chapter. When you implement a COA with built-in flexibility, you allow room for improvisation that will lead to the same desired outcome.

Redundancy

The last principle, redundancy, ensures safety nets are in place when a particular step in the COA isn't as effective as planned or fails completely. The aim of redundancy is to place copies of the same tangible or intangible resources to mitigate unforeseen factors and changes to the environment. For example, instead of only keeping one phone or one first aid kit in the bedroom closet, an emergency phone and first aid kit can be placed in the main-level bathroom and/or the kitchen. Moreover, parallel and duplicated efforts may be used to increase the likelihood of a successful plan, as even if one individual does not complete the task, the plan isn't completely unsuccessful, as the other individual may have more success in completing said task. Note: duplicated efforts do not need to be seen as mandatory since it may not be feasible depending on the number and capability of individuals involved.

Instead, it is a concept that is implemented when the situation and factors clearly present a reason for the strategy. For example, multiple people attempting to call 911 at once increases the likelihood of reaching an operator. Conversely, duplicating a search effort to retrieve people from a Safety Event may unnecessarily increase risk and complication for all parties involved.

Realism

Realism is the principle of tailoring COAs based on your current capabilities and resources. By referring back to your self-assessment, you will be able to realistically measure your abilities against a particular scenario. These will change over time as you work to improve your strengths and negate your limitations. You can adjust your COA due to your newfound capabilities and/or resources when it is appropriate. Be sure not to be too eager to throw in a new skill or resource too quickly, as doing so could lead to unnecessary uncertainty. Skill development, depending on the individual, can take weeks, to months, or even years to develop. So be sure to follow a training plan that develops the skill while also testing your proficiency. Once you have proven proficiency, the ability can be incorporated into your plan. The same is especially true for any resources you would like to implement.

For our purposes, I categorize resources as weapon systems, first aid treatments, security systems, communication systems, or any technology that you can utilize for your benefit during a Safety Event. I emphasize the importance of understanding and being proficient with your equipment, as certain equipment can be dangerous to the operating user if there is a lack of understanding and proficiency. The easiest example of this is firearms. If you would like to incorporate firearms into your Safety Plans, you must have proficiency in the weapon's safety, handling, and employment. Disregarding training increases risk of harm to yourself, your loved ones, and innocent bystanders. At the very least, you will be held legally liable for any action, purposeful or accidental. It is in your best interest if your actions are backed by training and sound decision-making. Other than weapon systems, it is important to train and use equipment that will be utilized in your Safety Plans to minimize the chances of malfunctions and user errors, especially when a particular COA relies on a particular resource to achieve a favorable outcome.

Backward Planning

The last concept of COA development we will use is backward planning. Backward planning is the same method of planning that we used to develop training curriculums and programs. Here, backward planning starts with the COA's end goal and works its way back to the first actionable step. Every COA you plan should begin with the four COA types stated before, although you could be specific to your exact situation. Once you know what risk you are mitigating and what desired outcome you want to plan for, you can formulate major movements that will take you back to the initiation of the plan.

Major movements should mirror sub-goals of the plan. Sub-goals can be to "retrieve first aid kit," "call 911," or "move to the family vehicle." Don't get caught up in the details of major movements initially, as we only want to create a general streamlined plan to basically get from point A to point B. Also, the details will more or less fall into place during the next step of planning. When backward planning, remember to follow the five guiding principles to keep the plan simple, quick, flexible, redundant, and realistic.

Figure 9 is an example of backward planning based on an active shooter situation at a shopping mall, while Figure 10 is an example of backward planning based on a home intruder scenario.

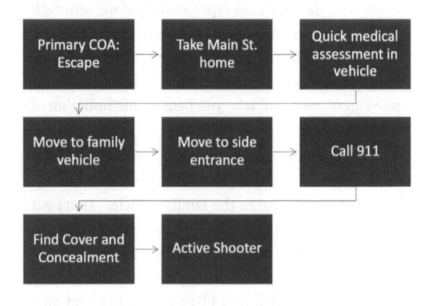

Figure 9: COA Active Shooter Backward Planning Example

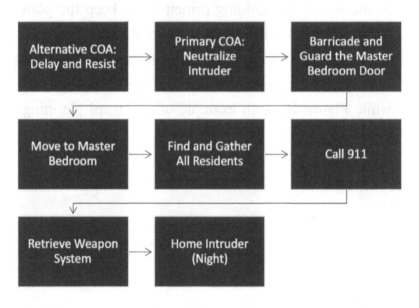

Figure 10: COA Backward Planning Home Invasion Example

As you can see, escape is the primary goal of the first COA, which is achieved by driving and traveling home in the family vehicle. The major movement that leads to arriving home includes the exact directions that will be taken. This was preceded by a medical assessment to ensure no medical intervention was needed, moving to the family vehicle together, moving to or meeting at the side entrance of the mall, calling 911 (if not under direct fire), and moving to cover and concealment once shots were fired. Each major movement has a direct link to the one before and after, with each serving an objective of maintaining safety and security until reaching the primary goal of the COA.

It may seem obvious when you write it down, but in the heat of the moment, there will be a lot of confusion and panic. The COA will help you keep it together when things get crazy.

Step 2: Contingency Planning

The last step in our planning process is something called contingency planning. Contingency planning is a way to make sure you have thought of every possible scenario. Similar to the Risk Tree Analysis, we will conduct a Decision Tree Analysis to assist with brainstorming possible scenarios. To narrow the scope, the tree should only consist of three branches per major movement, which detail scenarios based on best-case, worst-case, and mostly likely. Best-case scenario is when all the stars perfectly align, and you have every tool and all the needed resources available to successfully reach your goal. Worst-case scenario is when the offender is seen almost as invincible, and the deck has been stacked against you. Most likely scenario is, given all known facts, what any reasonable person would think would happen during a particular event. You can also add to the list of contingencies, but exploring these three scenarios is a good place to start. It not only provides a good range to plan for, but it also puts things into perspective. A lot of times we overexaggerate or understate due to the lack of perspective. Usually, when multiple perspectives are considered, we are able to alleviate stress and see situations more closely to the state of how they really are.

Active Shooter	Best-Case: Shooter will be stopped before initiating the attack.
	Worst-Case: Shooter will target us first.
	Most Likely: Shooter will initiate attack at an entrance to mall.
Find Cover and Concealment	Best-Case: Walls are made of brick and are within ten feet distance of us.
	Worst-Case: Walls are made of dry wall and are outside of fifty foot distance from us.
	Most Likely: Walls are made of brick and are within fifty foot distance from us.
Call 911	Best-Case: Personal cell phone has service and connects with 911.
	Worst-Case: Personal cell phone does not have service and there is no other phone in immediate area.
	Most Likely: Personal cell phone will have service and store will have a landline.
Move to Side Entrance	Best-Case: Side entrance is within a one minute run and unlocked.
	Worst-Case: Side entrance is on the other side of the mall and locked.
	Most Likely: Side entrance is within a two minute run and unlocked.
Move to Family Vehicle	Best-Case: Parking lot is clear of obstacles, vehicles, and pedestrians.
	Worst-Case: Parking lot is crowded by obstacles, vehicles, and pedestrians.
	Most Likely: Parking lot has typical amount of vehicles and pedestrians.
Quick Medical Assessment	Best-Case: No one has an injury.
	Worst-Case: Everyone has a life threatening injury.
	Most Likely: Minor injuries sustained (ex. sprained ankle)
Take Main St. Home	Best-Case: No traffic.
	Worst-Case: Heavy standstill traffic or road closure.
	Most Likely: Moderate traffic.

Figure 11: Contingency Plan Example

When looked at all at once, the Contingency Plan Example above can look busy and hard to follow. The goal is not to create a plan for each of the three cases but only to think through a realistic range of possible scenarios for each stage in the COA. As such, it is not necessary to look at the Figure as a series of events. Instead, you should view each major movement as its own element and establish the range of possible scenarios, starting with the best-case scenario and ending with the worst-case scenario. That range will then allow you to formulate the most likely scenario, as it will not fall out of the previously established range. The most likely scenario is the parameter your Safety Plan will follow.

COA development and contingency planning provides the practical framework for overall preparedness, creating safety habits, and maintaining a safety mindset. COA development is simply the act of finding possible solutions. While contingency planning ensures you think through all possible scenarios. The act and practice of thinking through the planning process will eventually transfer into real time problem-solving. However, a COA is never really tested unless actually implemented. This is why we must conduct rehearsals.

Chapter 15 Review

Points of Emphasis:

❖ "Failure to plan is planning to fail" and "Everyone has a plan until the bullets start flying" are both valid statements and warn against being ill-prepared for Safety Events.

❖ Safety Plans/Courses of Action (COA) are definitive solutions to Safety Events. Self-defense COAs should act to avoid threats, escape threats, neutralize threats, or delay and resist threats. COAs should be simple, timely, flexible, redundant, and realistic. COAs should only incorporate your current capabilities and resources.

❖ Contingency planning is formulating COAs based on potential scenarios that may arise. Contingency planning is based on analyzing possible factors to the worst-case, best-case, and most likely scenarios.

Perspective:

❖ Planning can get very detailed and very drawn out very quickly. No plan is perfect, and no amount of time planning is going to make it perfect. The key is having a plan, knowing the plan, and having the ability to enact the plan when needed. Remember, KISS—keep it stupid-simple. Or, if you prefer the original self-directed name calling version, keep it simple, stupid.

Call to Action:

☐ Complete the Safety Plan/COA Development Worksheet in the CTA Workbook.

☐ Create a Safety Plan/COA for:

☐ Home invasions

☐ Active shooter

☐ Kidnapping attempts

☐ Lost person recovery

☐ Any Safety Event that poses a threat to the safety of yourself and loved ones

Chapter 16:
Standard Operating Procedures

"In preparing for battle I have always found that plans are useless, but planning is indispensable."

Dwight D. Eisenhower

Standard Operating Procedures, more commonly referred to by the acronym SOPs, are preplanned operating templates. They can be derived from completed COAs, preestablished habits, or developed through efforts of trial and error. SOPs are universal solutions designed to fit many environments and situations. In businesses, this is the book of policies and procedures that no one ever reads but, ideally, are performed daily. SOPs can be implemented at an organizational level all the way down to the individual teams. The same is true in the military, which, in addition to administrative SOPs, also develops SOPs for military operations. SOPs for military operations are the building blocks for consistent, constant security, and control—no matter the mission set. To refine the concept,

I have separated types of SOPs by Action, Placement, and Security.

I'm sure you already have formulated SOPs pertaining to your daily schedule; they are probably just not written down. A very common example in everyday life is a family morning routine before going to work and school. During the morning routine, everyone usually has the same roles and responsibilities. One parent makes breakfast and gets the kids dressed. The other parent takes out the trash and cranks up the vehicles. During breakfast, everyone sits in their "assigned" seats. The trash can is placed on the right corner of the driveway for the trash service to pick it up. The kids make sure the pets are fed before gathering up their things for school. Spot has the brown food bowl, while Princess has the pink food bowl. When everyone leaves home for their respective places, the last person makes sure the front door is locked and secured. All done every morning of every day without contemplation or confusion—well, without mass confusion, anyway.

Action SOPs

This entire morning routine consists of multiple Action SOPs. Action SOPs are premeditated procedures for individuals that provide set roles and responsibilities. They can be elaborated to explain a sequence of events, but only if the events are universal. For example, in a Safety Event, a designated parent immediately regressing to the main bedroom to call the police is not an SOP. Instead, it is a specifically tailored plan for events at a place of residence, as it needs the elements of a bedroom (which is not universal to all situations). Rather, the SOP would look something like this: "Dad will call the police." Simple, precise, and universal. It can be further detailed as long as it can be applied in a home invasion, active shooter, motor vehicle accident, and so on.

As stated before, SOPs naturally derive from established COAs, as you will find patterns of action between different COAs. Through development, you will notice certain individuals are performing the same roles in different situations. As such, this should be solidified into an SOP and adjusted, if needed, to fit any situation. Additionally, there should be at least one person who can act as a backup during an Action SOP, meaning an individual, ideally someone who fits the CM profile, who could act as an alternative if the primary person is not present or is deemed encumbered. In addition to having a primary and alternate party to perform the action itself, there will also be PACE plan incorporated into the SOP in case of contingencies. The acronym PACE stands for primary, alternate, contingency, and emergency. Simply put, they are preplanned substitute elements of a COA that produce the same results. Figure 12 below shows an example of an Action SOP for calling 911.

Action SOP	Calling 911
Primary Party	Mom
Alternate Party	Dad
Primary Action	Use Mom's cell phone
Alternative Action	Use Dad's cell phone
Contingency Action	Use nearest landline
Emergency Action	Seek bystander and use their phone

Figure 12: Action SOP Example

As a recommendation to help you cover all your bases, I suggest assigning an individual who will always call the police, an individual who will always be the primary lead during an event, and an individual who will provide first aid if needed. Depending on the size of your household, one individual might have the honor of performing more than one of these responsibilities, or even all of them. Once you write down who's assigned to what, you can place it somewhere everyone can review it when need be. I suggest creating an SOP binder or notebook that can be placed on the family bookshelf, in a sofa table drawer, or perhaps in the junk drawer. Yes, I know about your junk drawer. If there isn't space in the junk drawer, make space—you don't need thirty old batteries and five half empty boxes of pens. You need an SOP book.

Placement SOPs

Those are just the people and assigned tasks, but odds are their tasks will involve a tool or device. This is where Placement SOPs come into play. Placement SOPs are premeditated procedures where equipment and supplies are placed in areas that are easily accessible and functionally appropriate. Think of a doctor who opens their medical cabinets—and every item has its assigned place, most likely labeled. Additionally, Placement SOPs can dictate position. Think of firefighters and first responders who automatically run to their assigned seats on their vehicles when responding to a call. Placement SOPs are important because they remove variability when needing a tool or piece of equipment. Anyone and everyone should know exactly where to look when searching for a critical piece of equipment. This helps with economy of motion, thereby saving time and energy, which is extremely important during Safety Events.

Any piece of equipment used for a Safety Event should have a Placement SOP of where and how it is securely stored, used, and implemented during an event. Figure 13 below shows an example of a Placement SOP when stocking a first aid bag. Labels or pictures of each item can also be used and placed on the bag itself. This helps ease the requirement of memorization and is especially helpful for kids. I also recommend a Placement SOP for keys for vehicles, home, and key locks; emergency gear such as fire extinguishers, flashlights, and communication devices; and most importantly for firearms, with specific consideration for keeping them quickly accessible but unattainable for children and unauthorized users.

Figure 13: First Aid Bag Placement SOP Example

Security SOPs

Lastly, we have the SOPs that are proactive in nature rather than reactive. Security SOPs are preventative SOPs that detail procedures that deter or prevent Safety Events from happening in the first place. These are usually simple tasks that prevent severe risks. Examples include locking your house doors, locking your vehicle doors, scanning your surroundings when first entering a new area, etc. All common tasks, but sometimes we take them for granted, and therefore, there are times we may forget to do them. They are especially critical when venturing outside your normal locations and routines. That said, we can become too complacent when an environment or situation becomes comfortable. If we feel comfortable in our home and neighborhood, we might forget to lock up. If we feel comfortable in a group of friends, we might not notice signs of danger or threatening person(s). In any situation, it is best practice to remain vigilant and secure with Security SOPs that take only a matter of seconds to complete and will prevent a whole mess of trouble.

SOPs are universal COAs in their simplest forms. Although they should be written down, placed in a binder or notebook, and reviewed monthly, they should also be easy to remember. Action SOPs outline "who does what." Placement SOPs outline "what is placed where." Security SOPs outline preventive measures. PACE plans embedded in SOPs ensure successful execution no matter what comes up in a situation. Once you have established SOPs, you can take a breath of liberation, as this is the last major step in planning and brainstorming. You can also breathe easier knowing that your established SOPs will assist you in any situation you may not have considered.

This is the beauty of SOPs. You don't need to be a Nostradamus and predict the future. You don't need an elaborate grand master plan that could rival plots of action-packed Hollywood movies. You only need

Standard Operating Procedures. Simple...boring... effective.

Chapter 16 Review

Points of Emphasis:

- ❖ Standard Operating Procedures (SOPs) are universal preplanned operating templates. SOPs are designed to fit various scenarios and should be the simplest forms of COAs.
- ❖ Action SOPs are premeditated procedures for individuals that provide set roles and responsibilities in response to a Safety Event. Examples are calling the police, providing first aid, escaping high-stress situations, actions taken when a child is separated from family in public, etc.
- ❖ Placement SOPs are premeditated procedures to place equipment and supplies in areas that are easily accessible and functionally appropriate. Examples are placement and safekeeping of firearms, loadout and placement of first aid kit, vehicle loadout and individual placement, etc.
- ❖ Security SOPs are preventative SOPs that detail procedures that deter or prevent Safety Events from happening. Examples include securing your home and vehicles, scanning new environments, having a "safe word" or "safe sign" when out in public with a group, etc.

Perspective:

❖ SOPs can be seen as a type of habit. As such, any SOP developed should follow as closely as possible the practices and habits you and your loved ones already follow. Start small and build upon easily maintainable habits.

Call to Action:

☐ Complete the SOP Development Worksheet in the CTA Workbook.

☐ Recommended Action SOPs are based on:

☐ Calling 911

☐ Group communication during a Safety Event

☐ Providing first aid

☐ Weapon employment

☐ Recommended Placement SOPs are based on:

☐ First aid kit loadout and placement

☐ Weapons and firearms storage and accessibility

☐ Recommended Security SOPs are based on:

☐ Securing your car and personal belongings when getting in and out of a vehicle

☐ Securing your home when leaving home, arriving home, and before bed

☐ Scanning a new environment for exits, suspicious people, and vantage points

Chapter 17:
Rehearsals

"The best time to practice mental rehearsal is at night in bed, just before you fall asleep. The last thing you do before you doze off is to imagine yourself performing at your best the following day. You will be amazed at how often the upcoming event or experience happens exactly as you imagined it."

Brian Tracy

After all the analytical work, brainstorming, and personal development, it is finally time to bring everything together for rehearsal. You have identified the skills, capabilities, and available resources that meet the Expertise Criteria, you have evaluated and considered relevant external factors, you have conducted risk assessments on possible threats, you have developed complete Safety Plans/COAs with relative SOPs. And after all that, you still have to test the product to make sure it works. And if it works, you have to continue to practice it to maintain effectiveness and readiness.

Basically, rehearsals are where the rubber meets the road and what makes a plan a definite plan. Writing a plan to paper increases your preparedness to about 10 percent. Rehearsal will bump that up to at least 90 percent. The last 10 percent is your mental fortitude. So, it goes without saying, rehearsals are extremely important. There are three main types of rehearsals you will use: mental, verbal, and physical. Each builds upon the other, but separately they provide their own unique benefits in maintaining readiness.

Mental rehearsals are essentially daydreams of a specific scenario. I assume most people daydream about spending time with a crush, on vacation, becoming a professional athlete, or winning the lottery. Although they may be a less pleasant type of daydreaming, mental rehearsals of a Safety Plan assist in overall preparedness and readiness. A significant benefit of mental rehearsals is that they can be done anywhere without others or equipment. You can run through a mental rehearsal at the gym, in the bathroom, on a car ride, while on a walk, or during another one of your boss's productivity meetings (just kidding...or am I?). Additionally, mental rehearsals provide opportunities to explore all contingencies and scenarios. Mentally rehearse for a home invasion of one individual, multiple individuals, or individuals with weapons—hell, you could mentally rehearse for a home invasion where the invaders are characters from your favorite horror movie. Nothing like defending your home from Jason and the Predator to make mental rehearsals a bit more interesting.

The last benefit of mental rehearsals is the fact that the mental task can be performed perfectly. This is the same principle addressed in Chapter 5: visualization. We know that by thinking through a task or series of tasks, we can create those same neurological connections as if it was physically performed. That's a lot of benefit for only "daydreaming." However, because of the ease of this type of rehearsal, overindulgence may ensue. Mental rehearsals are deliberate practices, not random thoughts. Treat them the same as you would any other physical training session or practice by setting a time and place when mental rehearsals will be conducted. Personally, I like running through a quick mental rehearsal before bed.

Taking it another step further would be conducting a verbal rehearsal. Verbal rehearsals are similar to reading a play or Hollywood movie script. Each step of your Safety Plan is read aloud to yourself or others. Preferably, everyone who is a part of the plan will read their portion of the plan. It should follow the sequence and can be the full scenario or just a segment of it. Verbal rehearsals can be conducted in the car, during family dinner, before bed, or at a dedicated family meeting. It can also be a question-and-answer session, especially if you have younger kids. Younger kids will stay interested if they believe it is a game, so it is best to present it as such. If you live alone, feel free to speak through your Safety Plans with friends and family. This third party can help audit your plan and also help create "what if" scenarios to ensure you are thinking of all realistic possibilities. The benefit of verbal rehearsals is that they are a way to internalize your Safety Plan while ensuring it is realistic, practical, and comprehensive.

Physical rehearsals are the ideal rehearsal type, and they *cannot* be neglected. I repeat, they CANNOT be neglected. Excuse my theatrics. All prevention techniques and Safety Plans are not validated until performed physically in real time. This is the only way to ensure confidence, efficiency, and pragmatism while conducting a Safety Plan in response to a Safety Event. Physical rehearsals should include all parties and resources utilized during a Safety Plan. There are two main types of physical rehearsals we will implement: the walk-through and talk-through, and the full dress rehearsal.

The walk-through and talk-through is the bridge between verbal and physical rehearsals. Instead of just reading through the plan, you will shadow each step as you are reading through it. Like before, you can either have one narrator who reads while each party performs their task, or you can have each party narrate and perform their tasks simultaneously. Walk-throughs and talk-throughs will be done at a moderate pace, as there is still an opportunity to work out any kinks. You will probably find yourself adjusting your plan, and this is a good thing. You will find that based on known, unknown, and ever-changing factors, plans need to be adjusted. Often, elements that sound good on paper don't translate well into the physical world, or they just need a slight adjustment. Refinement is progress, not an obstacle.

Lastly, we have the full dress rehearsal. This is the final practice before the big show. Well, hopefully not. Hopefully, the show never goes on, but that's how the dress rehearsal should be treated. Different from every rehearsal leading up to this point, it should be performed in real speed—meaning, the speed at which it would be performed during a real event. Mistakes will happen, but don't stop the rehearsal—adapt, and continue. Only after the rehearsal is completed will you sit down and evaluate the run—this is called an After-Action Review (AAR). AARs will allow you to dissect elements of the plan that were adjusted, missed, or worked well. Keep what works and throw out what doesn't. Repeat the dress rehearsal as many times as needed until there is no question that everyone knows what to do, when to do it, and how to do it. This does not mean subjecting your loved ones to grueling bouts of rehearsal-reset mayhem. It only means conducting the dress rehearsal as many times as needed so all parties know their Action SOPs and all equipment is placed according to the Placement SOPs. Once a plan has been vetted and validated, you can revisit it monthly or after elements of the plan change due to internal or external factors, i.e., new resources become available, kids leave for college, or a super creepy guy moves in next door.

Besides the three main types of rehearsals, there are numerous ways of conducting a rehearsal. A rehearsal can follow an entire scenario or just a segment of it. Rehearsals can be done alone, with others who are part of the plan, or with a third party. Rehearsals can be stopped and reset when a mistake is made, or they can continue on in real time. However conducted, there must be a reason for it: mainly, to ensure you have a valid functioning plan. But anything less than a full dress rehearsal should have an alternative goal that fits in with the overall goal of validating and solidifying your Safety Plan. For example, conducting a mental, segmented rehearsal of applying hemorrhage control allows you to think through the problem set in a low-stress environment without complication.

Note: a Home Invasion Safety Plan is the only plan that can be rehearsed as a full-dress rehearsal with complete freedom of movement and limited restrictions. This is one of the reasons it's been used as such a common example in this book. Other plans, such as those for active shooters and those in public spaces, cannot facilitate full dress rehearsals. As such, they are better suited for walk-throughs and talk-throughs, since conducting a full-dress rehearsal in the middle of a shopping mall would produce unwanted attention and a multitude of problems. Additionally, if firearms and other weaponry are part of your Home Invasion Safety Plan, before rehearsal, ensure all firearms do not contain ammunition and are handled with the same safety consideration as if they are loaded with ammunition. Safety during a rehearsal is the top priority, and every precaution must be taken to prevent injury.

It's vital that rehearsals are revisited on a frequent basis—and yes, I know, many things in this book are "vital." This is about life-or-death situations, after all. Anyway, it is vital, so I recommend doing one a month at a minimum. A rehearsal last conducted three months ago is likely to be ineffective or irrelevant today. All skills and elements of a Safety Plan are perishable. Even though riding a bike after years of not riding is doable, there still is an adjustment period where you wobble a bit before you get back into the swing of things. The same applies here. The difference is, these Safety Plans are meant to save your life, so you don't have the luxury of second tries. If you fall off your bike, you can hop back up and keep pedaling. If you fail to properly execute your Safety Plan, you risk never getting back up again. Rehearse your plans, and your plans won't fail you.

Chapter 17 Review

Points of Emphasis:

❖ Rehearsals are a method of working through, validating, and solidifying planned COAs.

❖ The three main types of rehearsals are mental, verbal, and physical.

❖ Mental rehearsals are conducted individually and through mental imagery.

❖ Verbal rehearsals are conducted as a group and serve as a method to speak through the planned COA.

❖ Physical rehearsals are conducted individually or as a group and serve as a method to form "muscle memory" or security habits.

Perspective:

❖ Rehearsals may seem corny and awkward at first, but they are conducted at the highest levels of any profession. The most significant and relevant examples would be those of military operations. The most elite military units rehearse constantly to ensure SOPs are developed, COAs are vetted, and to increase unit effectiveness.

Call to Action:

☐ At a minimum, conduct one mental rehearsal per week for five to ten minutes. This can be a rehearsal of an entire plan, specific sections or aspects of a plan, or a specific skill that is used during a plan.

☐ At a minimum, conduct one verbal rehearsal individually or as a group once a month. This can be a rehearsal of an entire plan, specific sections or aspects of a plan, or talking through a learned skill.

☐ At a minimum, conduct one physical rehearsal with all individuals involved in the plan once every three month. If rehearsing a Home Invasion Safety Plan, you can conduct a full dress rehearsal. Conduct walk-throughs and talk-throughs for all other Safety Plans. An AAR should be conducted at completion.

☐ Review and follow the Rehearsal/Scenario-based Training Checklist in the CTA Workbook.

End-of-Section Review

In this section, we reviewed risk assessment and analysis; formulating courses of action (COA), contingencies, and Standard Operating Procedures (SOPs); and the different types of rehearsals. Risk assessment and analysis identifies risks that require deliberate consideration and mitigation. COA, contingencies, and SOPs are methods of comprehensive mitigation and readiness. Rehearsals validate the strategies and actions of the COAs and SOPs. Although not a true implementation, as it is simulated, rehearsals can be classified as the last steps in the problem-solving cycle, as it is the implementation of the COA (Step 5) and facilitates the ability to adjust and adapt the COA as needed, which is the final step in the process.

At this point, you have all the necessary tools to prepare yourself and your loved ones for any event. And I mean *any*, as every concept introduced is designed to fit any situation you may find yourself in.

Section Four:
The Safety Event

"I'm scared every time I go into the ring, but it's how you handle it. What you have to do is plant your feet, bite down on your mouthpiece, and say, 'Let's go.'"

Mike Tyson

It always happens when you least expect it. What was once a normal day turns into chaos in a matter of seconds. There is no time for indecisiveness. No time for emotion. No time for "what if." The problem is right in front of you, right now, and it's time to face it head-on.

If you have ever asked anyone in the military a question on tactics, odds are the answer was simply "METT-TC." METT-TC stands for mission, enemy, terrain and weather, troops and support, time, and civilian consideration. When translated to civilian, it means "it depends." It is essentially all the listed factors that need to be considered before a specific strategy can be set and implemented. And within all those factors are many other elements of consideration that need to be analyzed before a course of action can be established. Yes, I know it's frustrating when you do not get an answer to a simple question that may indeed have a simple solution. But the fact of the matter is that self-defense tactics are not a one-size-fits-all product. Instead, and as you have seen so far, it is very detailed, very calculated, and requires extensive consideration.

This section is intended to introduce concepts affecting self-defense and Safety Events and provide models and guidance on them. This section does not provide specific details, techniques, or methodologies on how to counteract threats, as many of those need more extensive interactions to gain comprehension and development, which cannot be gained by reading a book. Not to mention the fact that there are an infinite number of real and potential scenarios to cover. Instead, this section is narrowed down to universal principles that only need a general understanding in order to be applied. These principles can be considered good "rules of thumb" that provide real time guidance during Safety Events.

Chapter 18:
Fight, Flight, Freeze

"Our training pushes us to develop a new set of instincts: instead of reacting to danger with a fight-or-flight adrenaline rush, we're trained to respond unemotionally by immediately prioritizing threats and methodically seeking to defuse them. We go from wanting to bolt for the exit to wanting to engage and understand what's going wrong, then fix."

Chris Hadfield

At the beginning of the book, I spoke about how gaining skill through experience in self-defense is difficult to do unless you have military or law enforcement experience. Oddly enough, although you may not have experienced a self-defense event (hopefully, you have not), you have experienced the same autonomous response that is enacted during a perceived stressful situation. When something unexpected or frightening happens, the body's immediate reaction is to attack it, run away from it, or lock up entirely. The response is so strong and fast you often don't get a choice which of the three you get. This is commonly referred to as the fight, flight (or flee), or freeze response. You might have already been introduced to the concept, as it is sometimes covered when referring to situations that induce stress, such as public speaking, being frightened by a jump scare, or even when a crush comes to speak to you for the first time. In this chapter, we will develop a deeper understanding of fight, flight, or freeze, and learn how to train your body to limit the effects so as to mitigate the occurrence during a real Safety Event.

The first time I was shot at on deployment, I only had a second of pause before I continued on with what I was doing. Chalk it up to training. I do believe my quick transition back to a state of calm, instead of a prolonged freeze, was based on the training and preparation I received. However, a couple weeks later, we were engaged by the enemy and my response was a little more severe. Instead of a slight pause, my initial reaction was that of my heart dropping into my stomach and me immediately ducking into cover behind the nearest truck. This time around, my response was about five seconds long, give or take, before I regained my composure and carried on.

I bring this up because anyone would assume that the first time you deal with a high-stress event would be the most severe fight, flight, or freeze response. However, the truth is, it varies depending on the situation. The first time I was shot at wasn't a surprise; we already knew there was fighting happening in the area, so my mindset was prepared for it. The other time, it was dead quiet before a sudden barrage of bullets began flying around me. But in any case, I was able to refocus on the task at hand, due to my training and preparation.

Knowing how this response works is crucial to learning how to mitigate its effect on you. Fight, flight, and freeze are the three possible autonomous reactions to a stimulus. The stimuli could be a real or perceived threat. This is important to understand, since we can only control our perception of a stimulus and not our central nervous system's response to the stimulus. Having a more complete perspective of a Safety Event assists in our ability to affect our body's state, no matter how little it may be. But trust me, any little bit helps.

At all times, we are either in a parasympathetic state or a sympathetic state. The parasympathetic state is generally referred to as "rest and digest." As the phrase suggests, this is when the body's systems are in a state of rest. This includes your resting heart rate, resting breathing rate, and resting blood pressure. Blood is being pumped primarily to internal organs, and your body is maintaining a hormonal balance optimal for rest.

A sympathetic state, referred to as the fight, flight, or freeze response, is the state where body systems react to and prepare for danger. Generally, this means an increased heart rate, increased breathing rate, and increased blood pressure. Blood is diverted from the digestive tract to your musculoskeletal system, and there is a release of adrenaline.

Fight is the autonomic reaction to directly engage the threat. *Flight* is the autonomic reaction to flee from the threat. *Freeze* is the autonomic reaction of a type of paralytic state where the body is unable to move.

The goal is to train your mind to quickly refocus back to a state of conscious control once that sympathetic state has been activated. This is done in two ways: exposure and focus training.

The first way is through exposure. The more we are exposed to a particular stimulus, the less of a chance of a prolonged autonomic response. For example, our first response to hearing a loud noise might be a flinch, then fear, confusion, and finally resolve. If we hear that loud bang enough times, we still may flinch, but odds are the fear and confusion will be drastically reduced, as our minds understand now where the loud bang might be coming from. This type of exposure has caused the sympathetic response to be less severe.

As is the case with self-defense, experience may only be gained through simulation. These simulations are usually referred to as scenario-based training and do provide the same benefits as real-life experience, just like our rehearsals. I am a huge proponent of scenario-based training, as it provides valuable insight second only to real-world events. However, scenario-based training—and some types of exposure to self-defense practices—should only be performed in controlled environments with multiple layers of safety consideration, usually facilitated by professionals of that particular field.

Beyond exposure, there is refocusing. Refocusing is the same concept we learned in Chapter 5 where we reviewed the practice of distraction awareness. The same principle is applied here, as the "distraction" we are attempting to mitigate is our own body's response. It is not the stimulus—the stimulus is what we need to be focused *on*, as it is the perceived threat. Refocusing is done through mindful breathing and awareness of the space around us, the perceived threat, and our position in relation to the perceived threat. Mindful breathing eases the sympathetic response by stimulating the vagus nerve, which helps regulate heart rate, breathing rate, and blood pressure. Awareness brings clarity of the situation so the brain can begin to make rational decisions based on better perceived information. Both will ease the effects of your sympathetic nervous system and will give you an opportunity to react in a more focused, deliberate manner. Obviously, this is way easier said than done in the heat of the moment, but that's why practicing it is essential. If you can do it enough times in a calm, controlled environment, you'll be able to do the same when the environment is a bit more chaotic.

Overall, our sympathetic nervous system is not harmful nor counterproductive, as it serves an important role in survival. However, since it doesn't know how to properly discriminate between types of threats and the best COA in counteracting that threat, it must be alleviated enough for the use of higher cognitive functions. You can think of your sympathetic nervous system as the spark plug that starts the engine, but you still need to take the wheel and control how fast and where the vehicle will go. Runaway vehicles are a danger to others and its occupants, but a Ferrari in the hands of a seasoned racecar driver can get you where you're going—*fast*.

Chapter 18 Review

Points of Emphasis:

❖ Your response to real or perceived danger will initiate an autonomic response controlled by your sympathetic nervous system. This response will be to either fight, flee, or freeze.

❖ Although designed to physiologically prepare you for danger, if not managed, this sympathetic response may hinder your ability to adequately protect yourself.

❖ Exposure and focus training are two ways to lessen the unwanted effects of fight, flight, or freeze. Exposure, through experience and scenario training, increases our overall understanding of the stimulus, which decreases the effect it has on us. Refocusing, through mindful breathing and awareness, counteracts the sympathetic nervous system through physiological means.

Perspective:

❖ The human body and its functions are truly an engineering wonder. Unfortunately, sometimes our body doesn't know when the "help" it is providing is actually harmful, like in the cases of high fevers, allergies, and sometimes when responding to danger. In regard to fight, flight, or freeze, the key is not to attempt to get rid of it completely but to harness it to produce better results.

Call to Action:

☐ Anytime you feel yourself in a stressful situation, practice mindful breathing. Refocus your awareness back to your mental, physical, and emotional state and your surroundings.

☐ Based on your Safety Goals and supporting tasks, identify skills/elements that can be simulated through scenario-based training. Examples include verbal altercations and de-escalation, assault attempts and combatives, firearms and live shooting at a gun range, etc.

☐ Implement scenario-based training in your skill development programs. Review the Rehearsal/ Scenario-Based Training Checklist in the CTA Workbook to assist you in adding it to your programming.

Chapter 19:
Types of Safety Events

"Violence, even well intentioned, always rebounds upon oneself."

Lao Tzu

Knowing the type of incident that is occurring makes deciding on a course of action easier, thereby increasing survivability. Some might believe that an attack is an attack no matter how it happens. However, just as a boxer blocks and counters a specific punch based on whether it's a jab, hook, or cross, we must act in the same way. We are not able to analyze every specific detail with each scenario, as there are infinite elements to infinite scenarios. But we are able to review the framework each incident follows, which provides distinct elements for consideration and counteraction. The type of Safety Events we will cover are ambushes, raids, escalations, and indiscriminate incidents, along with SOP and COA considerations for each.

Ambushes

An ambush is usually known as an attack by surprise from a hidden place. The most popular example of an ambush would be any war movie where one military force attacks another's patrol from hidden positions in a jungle as the patrol unknowingly walks into danger. However, an ambush does not need to be from a hidden place. In fact, more times than not, it will be in plain sight of public view. Think of the recent string of random attacks in large cities, where the criminal casually walks up to people and punches them or purse snatchers with their snatch-and-run strategy. The key elements for consideration are the element of surprise, the quick access, and the eventual goal of fleeing the scene. The element of surprise is the ability to attack unbeknownst to others and is the most significant advantage the aggressor has. The quick access is the aggressor's ability to attack unimpeded, meaning the aggressor is within close distance with no obstacles hindering their movement. Lastly, the aggressor does not remain in the area once the ambush is completed or counteracted. So, the goal would be to flee as quickly as possible. Aggressors who use ambush as a tactic do not want a prolonged attack. They want to commit violence, or another criminal activity, as fast as possible and leave as fast as possible, thereby increasing the chances of accomplishing their objective and getting away with it. When met with counteraction of high intensity, it is likely the aggressor will flee immediately. This is due to the fact that ambushes are meant for targets of least resistance or individuals who seem to be defenseless. If they do happen to continue the attack, prioritize your COAs based on escape, neutralization, and lastly, delaying and resisting.

Action SOPs utilized to counter ambushes should emphasize violence of action. Violence of action is a military term that describes accurate, speedy, and forceful aggressive action aimed at an enemy that provides the enemy no chance of counter or defense. Essentially, it's going zero to one hundred and keeping it at a level of one hundred until the enemy has been subdued or flees. Another way of putting it is your sports team is down by one score with only ten seconds left in the game. If they want to win the game, they are going to have to pull out the one play that is known to work no matter who they are playing.

Applied to an ambush, an Action SOP that emphasizes violence of action ensures you are using your top strengths and resources as quickly as possible until your risk of harm is as close to zero as possible. This means your Placement SOPs should enable the violence of action, meaning placing any resource (firearm, pepper spray, other defense tools) in a way that enables quick employment. If it takes you more than a couple of seconds (more than two seconds is pushing it) to find and use that particular resource, it is not a viable Placement SOP for counteracting an ambush.

Raids

A raid is an attack at a physical location where the aggressor plans to withdraw afterward—or expire in place, as in the cases of suicide or "suicide by cop." The distinction between a raid and an ambush is the element of physical structures. Ambushes do not have physical barriers hindering the attacker's ability to reach the intended targets. Raids, on the other hand, do have the element of physical barriers, which hinder the attacker's freedom of movement. Examples of raids include home invasions, active shooters, store robberies, etc. The key elements of a raid are entry, internal maneuvering, and withdrawal.

Entry is the action of accessing a physical location, which could be done with or without force. An attack cannot be initiated unless the aggressor gains entry. Obvious, yes, but still an important consideration, as it means if they can be denied entry, the raid may never take place at all.

Internal maneuvering refers to the actions within the physical location. This can be static or dynamic, meaning the aggressor could run all over the place or just simply find an area and act to control only a section of the larger physical location.

The last step in the raid is the withdrawal. As stated before, this could mean the aggressor flees the location, commits suicide, or provokes "suicide by cop."

Due to the element of a physical location, Action SOP consideration for raids involve moving in space while utilizing physical structures, barriers, and resources. If not in direct engagement by the aggressor, Action SOPs would be utilized to support avoidance and escape. For example, an Action SOP may dictate what escape route to use by either immediately finding the emergency stairwell or sticking to the outside parameter of an area behind cover until you reach an exit. Similarly, an Action SOP may dictate how you maneuver throughout the area, whether one by one or in groups. If in direct engagement from the aggressor, Action SOPs would be utilized to either enact violence of action or to find cover, depending on the distance from the aggressor and resources available. If the physical location is your home, your Home Invasion Safety Plan should be enacted along with the relevant SOPs.

Placement SOPs can be utilized to maintain personnel accountability and availability of resources during a raid. For example, to maintain communication with others, a Placement SOP might dictate that everyone within your party must have a phone with a "push to talk" app, a mobile app that acts similar to a "push to talk" radio, or have a group conference call already preestablished. Additionally, a Placement SOP could be established for easy-access placement of a first aid kit in the family vehicle.

Escalations

More subtle than ambushes and raids, escalations are events where the aggressor has established contact before initiating an attack. This can happen in two ways: either with premeditated intentions or an emotional response. Premeditated escalations are when the aggressor has permitted access to an individual and initiates an attack due to opportunistic conditions. An example of this is in the cases of rape or sexual assault where the aggressor may act within social norms but turn aggressive when their potential victim is most vulnerable. You see this often with casual meetings at bars and other social events. Two people are enjoying each other's company, but then things go south once alone and one of them reveals their true ill intentions. In a way, it is similar to an ambush, since the attack itself is seemingly initiated by surprise. However, the difference is the permissible access the aggressor gained before initiating the attack. In an ambush, the aggressor does not have permissible access. Just to be clear, permissible access is when we allow individuals into our personal space, whether physical, mental, or emotional. In the case of two people meeting at the bar, the predator is looking to gain that access to get past their victim's defenses, so their attack is met with the least amount of resistance possible.

Emotional escalations are events that often begin benign and turn violent due to emotional influence, such as arguments, bar fights, road rage, etc. Generally, emotional escalation incidents follow continuing stages of escalation that present opportunity(s) to prevent the event from reaching a point of violence. In this type of incident, both the aggressor and potential victim have generally the same understanding of the event and watch it play out in real time concurrently. This dynamic causes an even plane where no party necessarily has an upper hand unless they are better skilled or better prepared.

Action SOPs utilized to mitigate escalation events, or those that follow a series of events that may result in acts of violence, should emphasize de-escalation, avoidance, and escape. This is due to the nature of the threat. With ambushes, the threat is clear and imminent and should be met with proportionate force. With escalation events, the threat may be present but not necessarily imminent. Therefore, the most favorable outcome is achieved through nonviolent means. However, once the threat turns imminent it should be met with violence of action.

Depending on your involvement—either direct contact or indirect contact with an aggressor—de-escalation is used to resolve the event or buy time until law enforcement arrives at the scene. If not directly involved, be careful about stepping in too quickly if you do not have enough information to act or have not been trained in de-escalation techniques. In some escalation events, adding too many variables causes the event to escalate more rapidly. Instead, it would be more beneficial to position yourself where you can act if the event does become violent, whether to subdue the offender, protect a victim, or escape the situation.

Indiscriminate Incidents

Indiscriminate incidents are those that happen due to natural occurrences, unintelligible processes, and otherwise unlucky sets of circumstances. These events can be motor vehicle crashes, earthquakes, fires, animal attacks, storms, and accidental harm. The characteristics of random incidents are neglectfulness, haphazardness, and the absence of a motive or malicious intent. The key differentiation from the other three events is that indiscriminate incidents are chaotic in nature and do not target individuals. Since there can be many uncontrollable factors in random incidents, there is more of an emphasis on avoidance and escape rather than de-escalation or attempting to counteract the event.

Humans can sometimes be reasoned with—nature, not so much. Any COA or SOP that pertains to indiscriminate incidents should emphasize simplistic routes to safety, control of the people involved, as well as logistical considerations for food, water, and medical supplies.

Ambushes, raids, escalations, and indiscriminate incidents all act differently, but all result in the same outcome when not counteracted or mitigated. They are a means to an end, but that end is to your detriment. As such, knowing how they act provides you with the ability to know how to counteract them. Although there are specific SOP and COA considerations depending on the elements of each, you should start to see how it all fits a common theme.

Self-defense is reacting to dynamic, violent, and chaotic situations with accustomed tactics to simplify the focus of the problem. When we do that, the problem becomes less about reaction and more about getting to work and implementing the solution.

Chapter 19 Review

Points of Emphasis:

❖ The four distinct types of Safety Events are ambushes, raids, escalations, and indiscriminate incidents.

❖ An ambush is a surprise attack with no preestablished contact with the victim. The key elements for consideration are the element of surprise, the quick access, and the eventual goal of fleeing the scene. Action SOPs that counter ambushes should emphasize violence of action.

❖ A raid is an attack at a physical location where the aggressor plans to withdraw or expire in place, as in the cases of suicide or "suicide by cop." The key elements of a raid are the entry, internal maneuvering, and withdrawal. Action SOPs that counter raids should emphasize maneuvering safely, control of the people involved, and violence of action if needed.

❖ Escalations are events where the aggressor has established contact before initiating an attack, either with premeditated intentions or an emotional response. The key element of escalations are the opportunities to prevent violence through de-escalation or avoidance. Action SOPs should emphasize positioning yourself out of harm's way while utilizing de-escalation techniques.

❖ Indiscriminate incidents are those that happen due to natural occurrences, unintelligible processes, and otherwise unlucky sets of circumstances. Any COA or SOP that pertains to indiscriminate incidents should emphasize simplistic routes to safety, control of the people involved, as well as logistical consideration for food, water, and medical supplies.

Perspective:

❖ Although ambushes and raids are usually associated with military operations, their elements can be translated for self-defense—for what are military operations if not just offensive attacks and defensive counters on a large scale? As such, understanding the elemental foundation to military defensive tactics provides insight on individual protection and self-defense.

Call to Action:

- ☐ Review SOPs created from Chapter 16 and ensure at least one can be implemented when reacting to each type of Safety Event based on their SOP considerations:
    - ☐ Ambush—violence of action
    - ☐ Raid—maneuvering, group control, violence of action
    - ☐ Escalation—safety positioning, de-escalation techniques, violence of action
    - ☐ Indiscriminate Incident—means and ways of getting to safety, group control, logistical placement

Chapter 20:
Four Principles of Survival

"Survival can be summed up in three words: never give up. That's the heart of it really. Just keep trying."

Bear Grylls

Confusion runs rampant during chaos. Of course, we already know this. This is why we started implementing focus training as a part of our training programs. (...Right?) But we can also help ourselves out during a Safety Event by relying on basic concepts that can be easily recalled to increase survivability. Together, these concepts are what I call the Four Principles of Survival and they are SOP implementation, layered security, control, and common sense. The principles are ordered in a way that prioritizes preplanned measures. They may blend together, too, as they are two sides of the same coin—or rather, four sides of the same square. For example, layered security can be predesigned by SOPs, the implementation of SOPs provides a certain level of control, and all should follow the principle of common sense. Nonetheless, they should be considered individually during an event to ensure all risks are mitigated. The four principles also form the acronym SLCC (pronounced slick), which provides a nice way of recall—since you'll need to be slick in order to come out of the Safety Event unharmed.

The Four Principles of Survival is the civilian's equivalent to the Army's Five Principles of Patrolling, which outline key principles every patrol should follow to conduct a mission successfully. These principles include planning, reconnaissance, security, control, and common sense. The Army's principles provide overarching guidance to units to increase mission success and survivability from the receipt of a mission until the return to home base. However, considering the Five Principles of Patrolling are based on military operation, it doesn't make much practical or legal sense to utilize it for everyday life. Besides, if you have followed the recommendations of this book so far, you have already conducted planning and reconnaissance—otherwise known as "research." I have left them out of the Four Principles of Survival, due to their preparatory purpose. The Four Principles of Survival are designed for real time events and are thus key concepts to focus on when needing to get out of a tight spot.

1. SOP implementation

As we went over previously, SOPs are meant to be universal, preplanned templates of specific actions, placements, or security measures. Utilizing your SOPs during a Safety Event is the baseline principle for survival, as it will increase the likelihood of gaining an advantage to avoid, escape, or neutralize the threat. That is, of course, if you are rehearsing your SOPs. If not, then they will be less effective. And in the case of not having one at all, your reaction to an event will likely be chaotic, erratic, and inefficient, which will lead to unmitigated risks. Fortunately, you are a responsible person of action, evident from the fact that you are currently reading this book, and you are maintaining a suitable level of preparedness and rehearsing your SOPs at least once a month. Therefore, they should be practically second nature when reacting to an incident, thereby serving as your foundation for survival.

2. Layered security

Next, we have layered security. Layered security is the concept of implementing multiple security measures all at once. Some of these security measures will be active, meaning you will actively be executing a task, and other measures will be passive, meaning they are always present without the need for human operation. Active security measures include all physical mitigation techniques, such as shouting, negotiation, physical restraint, weapon employment, and egression. Passive security measures include obstacles, security cameras, alarms, pet animals, or distance itself. Fences, doors, trees, walls, or anything that prevents direct alignment between you and an assailant(s) are all examples of obstacles. Layered security employs as many of these techniques as possible—the more, the better. As an example, layered security can look like the following: early warning devices such as cameras and alarms, distance from the offender(s), obstacles and cover between you and the offender, elevational perspective in relation to the offender(s), and any weapon systems being carried. As we covered before, sometimes the only thing needed to deter an attacker is impeding the speed and ease at which they can commit their crime.

3. Control

Control is the simple concept of the ability to maintain, well, *control.* Control can be seen from the perspective of the overall event itself, but in this case, we are only talking about control of yourself and your significant people. Internal control of yourself is the emotional and physical control you have developed through your training and preparation. External control is that of others, whether you're directing members of your Safety Plan or slowing an attacker. The sub-component of external control is communication, as communication is the driving force of external control. However, control of others can be through physical, verbal, or nonverbal means. Physical control is maintaining physical contact with another individual in order to guide them. Verbal control is the ability to speak and provide direction through means of audible conversation. Nonverbal control is the ability to gesture or utilize the environment as signals, which provides direction to others. We'll be focusing on the external control of those who are a part of our Safety Plans or may be bystanders who need assistance navigating the Safety Event.

Physical control is less ideal, as it limits your freedom of movement and ability to do other tasks. However, it is the most assured form of control. Verbal control, whether by a digital device or not, is more ideal, as you are able to provide direction and guidance while not needing to physically be near the individual(s). It is slightly less assured, as it's up to the individual receiving the verbal orders to interpret them, but with clear and concise directions, they should be able to understand what needs to happen. Lastly, we have nonverbal control, which is most ideal, as it is effective and efficient while being the least labor-intensive of the three. Text and other forms of digital messaging are forms of nonverbal communication but are only suited for events that do not pose immediate threat, as the method is too slow to keep up with quickly developing events. Other nonverbal communication can be arm and hand signals or perhaps just a glance of the eyes. These methods maintain control while utilizing efficient communication, all without being conspicuous. And yes, this is something that needs to be practiced through planning, establishing SOPs, and rehearsing.

The best example of nonverbal communication in a tactical situation is military foot patrols. When moving through hostile territory, military patrol relies on nonverbal communication, through hand and arm signals, to maintain noise discipline while also maintaining awareness of their surrounding area. Even with predetermined signals, it helps when everyone on patrol already knows their set roles and responsibilities along with established SOPs that are implemented based on encountered events. That way, the only communication that is needed is used to direct movement or warn others of danger. In its most basic form, nonverbal communication is distance, direction, and a simple point of the finger to indicate important information, such as, "enemy over there."

4. Common sense

Lastly, we have common sense. Arguably the most important principle of the four, it is also the most ambiguous—and yet, also the most straightforward. You may have heard that common sense is not common. This can be due to multiple factors, with the biggest one simply being confusion. In the heat of a high-pressure moment, it's easy to lose track of everything, including common sense. However, I believe that can be mitigated by asking two questions: first ask, "What's the obvious COA?" and secondly, "Is there any reason why I shouldn't do the obvious?" By asking those two questions, you will increase the likelihood of developing a simple solution while increasing the odds the solution will be implemented effectively and successfully. Common sense is nothing more than utilizing a sound decision-making process while not overcomplicating the already complicated situation. Planning and preparation will only make you faster at answering those two questions.

The Four Principles of Survival, SLCC, are key concepts that can be easily recalled in any situation to successfully achieve the goal of avoidance, escape, delay, and neutralization. Each concept can parallel the others or have a direct influence over one or many. Applied together, they are designed to mitigate any threat, in any scenario, no matter how chaotic. If you are ever in a Safety Event, just remember to breathe and be SLCC.

Chapter 20 Review

Points of Emphasis:

❖ The Four Principles of Survival provide basic concepts that can be recalled during an event to increase survivability. They are SOP implementation, layered security, control, and common sense, which can be recalled through the acronym SLCC.

❖ SOP Implementation is the principle of relying on your preestablished SOPs, which serve as the foundation to your security.

❖ Layered security is the principle of maintaining and implementing multiple security measures through passive and active means.

❖ Control is the ability to maintain personal control over your own physical, mental, and emotional state, as well as the control of other individuals who are part of your Safety Plan through physical, verbal, or nonverbal means.

❖ Common sense is the principle of not trying to overthink a situation and keeping strategies simple.

Perspective:

❖ Although coined as principles, SOP implementation, layered security, control, and common sense are *skills,* and should be practiced and developed—perhaps not in the traditional sense of conducting a "training session," but rather by implementing each principle into everyday life. For example, practice nonverbal communication with your family while doing chores around the house or think through passive and active security layering at different locations when running errands around town.

Call to Action:

☐ Review the COAs you developed in Chapter 15. Ensure they follow the Four Principles of Survival, SLCC, by utilizing SOPs, layers of security, methods of control, and common sense. Adjust if necessary.

Chapter 21:
Situational Awareness

"The better awareness, the better your choices. As you make better choices, you will see better results."

Anonymous

To refine our focus and be more than just an oblivious bystander, we'll need to sharpen our awareness. Awareness is the ability to maintain perception of your surroundings. Half the battle of avoidance and prevention is maintaining awareness, which is hard in this age of technology and smartphones. The other half of the battle is understanding what you are seeing, hearing, and even feeling. Most people believe you must be a veteran detective or super spy to be able to spot subtle signs of danger. In reality, anyone and everyone has the ability to do so. In fact, they already do it, every day of their lives. Due to human's past history of fending off predators and being in a constant state of survival, we still have the innate ability to spot any threat of harm. The key is to understand the context, identify the pattern, listen to your intuition, and stay logical. We'll be focusing on four general principles that will help us do just that.

The first principle is to understand the context. We all know what "normal" looks like, especially in our society. We are constantly exposed to societal norms and patterns, which makes it easy to spot things that are out of place. Context provides the rationale for when something is "normal" or when it is out of place. For example, an individual with a baseball bat creates two different scenarios just based on location and context. If the individual is near a baseball field, it is considered normal. So, it is likely they do not pose a threat even though baseball bats can be used as a deadly weapon. Now, if the same individual is walking around a commercial parking lot, well that's something to take notice of. In this case, the context does not fit, so we focus more attention to the baseball bat wielding-individual and begin to evaluate the potential threat based on the second principle.

The second principle is to identify the relationships between clues, whether subtle or obvious. As with most aspects of life, an individual factor does not provide the complete story. It is the presence of multiple factors and the relationship between them that provides the context needed in a self-defense scenario. One factor can be a coincidence, but a pattern is more likely to be deliberate action. With our baseball bat-wielding example, once we notice the abnormal, we then look for more clues as to the intention of this individual. We take notice of their facial expression, where they are looking, type of hand positioning on the bat, speed of which they are traveling, whether the bat is up in the air or down by their side. If they look angry, sporadically looking around, have a tight two-hand grip on the bat, walking at a brisk pace, and have the bat upright and ready to swing, well, we can make a determination that the individual likely has ill intent and it's time to implement a Safety Plan. If they look content, are looking ahead, one hand gripping the middle of the bat, walking at a leisurely pace, and have the bat down at their hip, then we can still keep an eye on them, but there would be little reason to enact a Safety Plan.

Be careful not to fall into confirmation bias where you begin to search for clues that "reach a conclusion" that fits your hypothesis of the situation. The process of awareness and analyzing a situation is inherently objective. Yet we are human, and as such, we maintain biases whether we like to or not. The key is to understand our biases so our analysis will more closely reflect the reality of the situation. We may become better attuned to analyze quicker and more accurately based on past experience, but there is always a chance confirmation bias sneaks into our analytical process. And it can go both ways—you may try to convince yourself a situation is dangerous when it really isn't, and in other cases, you may do the opposite and ignore a dangerous situation by convincing yourself that everything is all right. Notice the abnormal, objectively analyze the relationship between additional clues, and listen to your gut.

The third principle is to listen to your intuition, otherwise known as a "gut feeling." Intuition, an unexplained feeling and unconscious understanding, is one of the most valuable tools for your safety. It is often what guides our thoughts and actions once we notice something out of the ordinary. Once you have identified that something is out of place or odd, your intuition will cause your body to start to transition into a sympathetic state (the fight, flight, or freeze state). This unconscious analysis may not be able to pinpoint exactly why there is an issue, but your unconscious mind is trying to push you in the right direction. Depending on the details of the stimulus, people are inclined to resist their intuition so as not to seem rude or offensive. In the same way we do not want to establish confirmation bias, we also do not want to ignore our intuition. *The Gift of Fear* by Gavin de Becker goes over this in further detail, with excellent examples of various situations where intuition was actively trying to prevent threat of life and bodily harm.

Lastly, just as common sense is a Principle of Survival, it is a relevant principle when it comes to awareness and picking up warning signs. It can also be seen as simply staying logical when analyzing a situation. As we know, emotions have the ability to sway our analytical thinking. Common sense does not negate intuition. Common sense calibrates your response to the stimuli. In a sense, it is an example of Newton's Third Law, which states that for every action, there is an equal, opposite reaction. The simplest example of this is if a threatening person takes a step toward you, you should take a step away from them, to maintain the safe distance needed in layered security.

A more involved example would be if it seems as if a person is following you as you are leaving work. It could be a coincidence, or it could not. In this scenario, the threat is not immediate and is therefore perceived as a *potential* threat. The equal, opposite reaction to this scenario is that of precaution and proactiveness. You must first validate whether or not you are being followed before taking action to counteract the aggression. During the same time, you should remain in the car, continuing to drive—in populated areas— as your safety is maintained by both staying visible to the general public and by keeping up the physical separation caused by remaining in a moving vehicle. If you take a few turns and the car stops following you, you will have assurance of safety without having acted irrationally, by subtly testing the situation. If, however, the vehicle has taken enough turns where it's obvious their route is based on your actions, it is time to take more deliberate action by calling 911 and driving to the nearest police station. There is more to this example, but the principle I want you to understand is: when a potential threat is perceived, a plan should be enacted to ensure safety while gathering intelligence to guide the next steps of the plan.

Awareness is yet another simple skill that is hard to master. The key is to build a habit of remaining aware of your surroundings in your daily life while staying vigilant in situations where you may be more vulnerable, such as dimly lit environments, when you're alone in unfamiliar areas, etc. Essentially, you should maintain the same level of awareness when out in public as you do when driving a car: vigilantly looking front, left, right, and checking your mirrors for what's behind you, all while staying off your phone. Now, this doesn't mean that you can never check your phone out in public. However, if you find that after you stop using your phone you feel like you've "zoned out," or that you need to regain your bearings of your surroundings, that means you were on your phone for too long and were left vulnerable to your surroundings. Any vulnerability can be used as an advantage by an attacker, which is ground you will need to make up to gain an advantage. Maintaining awareness ensures you never will be caught off guard. As the saying goes, keep your head on a swivel and stay aware.

Chapter 21 Review

Points of Emphasis:

❖ Awareness is the ability to maintain perception of your surroundings. Specific to safety, awareness is also noticing things that are obviously or subtly "out of place," identifying the pattern, listening to your intuition, and staying logical.

❖ Most often, one clue will not provide the whole story or enough to act on. But if there is something to act on, odds are there are other clues that will show a pattern.

❖ Your intuition, otherwise known as your "gut feeling," should not be ignored when feeling unsafe. Do not be an apologist for others; instead, ensure your safety is the number one priority.

❖ Common sense calibrates your response to your perception of danger. If there's a perceived potential threat, take action to prevent and prepare for danger.

Perspective:

❖ Listen to your "gut," but rely on your problem-solving abilities. As intuition is the subconscious mind's reaction to a stimulus and problem-solving is the conscious process, both working together gives you the best chance to avoid and mitigate danger.

Call to Action:

- ☐ Establish a daily practice of awareness when in public.
    - ☐ Avoid prolonged phone usage or other distractions.
    - ☐ Take note of the social norms of individuals, groups, and how they all mesh in public.
    - ☐ Identify the "out of place", analyze for patterns, and mitigate risks as needed.

Chapter 22:
Tactical Advantage

"You win battles by knowing the enemy's timing, and using a timing which the enemy does not expect."

Miyamoto Musashi

As my experiences with military operations and combatives training has taught me, understanding how and being able to gain tactical advantage greatly increases the odds of a favorable outcome. Tactical advantage is the state of having greater ability to affect an opponent in relation to the effect they have on you through means of positioning, available resources, or reinforcement. Positioning is the tactic of placing yourself in an advantageous spatial relationship with a threat based on body positioning, distance, elevation, and environmental factors. Resources include equipment or weaponry that directly change the dynamic of the situation. Reinforcements are other individuals that act to further one's effort. In a simplified model, whoever has the support of all three elements has a tactical advantage. This can be achieved by four rules: force them to "play your game," establish leverage through positioning, build leverage through positioning and resources, and utilize leverage decisively through means of position, resources, and reinforcements.

Forcing them to "play your game" means manipulating the situation to play into your skills and strategies. This keeps you in a zone of clarity and clear direction, as you do not have to react and think through a brand-new problem set. Ideally, this is done through the implementation of your SOPs. By doing so, you know what should happen and when it should happen. Conversely, the offender is then put into a position where they must think through complex problem sets, expending time, effort, and resources just to regain tactical advantage. If your COA is to escape, you will systematically move from cover to cover until you find an avenue or means of escape. If your COA is to neutralize the threat, you will systematically move to cover that provides a clear, unobstructed view of (or approach to) the attacker. If you have no other choice but to resist and delay the attacker, you will look to find an area closed off from the attacker or will need to make a decision to engage the attacker with whatever resources available.

Note: although often used together, "cover" and "concealment" are two different things. Cover are objects or structures that can stop bullet penetration. Concealment are objects or structures that obscure your location. Going back to third-grade geometry, we know a square can be a rectangle, but a rectangle is not necessarily a square. A similar situation applies here. Cover, when large enough, can also be concealment, but concealment is not always cover. Bottom line, cover is a must have when bullets are flying.

Establishing leverage means gaining a foothold to build upon through reactive defensive maneuvers. This can be as direct as you grabbing an assailant before they can effectively attack you or by positioning yourself in an advantageous location relative to the attacker. Initial leverage is positioning meant to inhibit the offender's ability to employ effective attacks. If the attack is initiated hand-to-hand, this means positioning yourself on the attacker's body that immobilizes the attacker just enough to impede the attacker's accuracy, force, and control. Notice I said, "just enough." Immobilizing the attacker completely is ideal, but impeding their ability to effectively attack is the goal at this stage.

If the attack is initiated with a firearm, positioning is based on the distance between you and the shooter, the elevation of both you and the shooter, and any obstacles in the area. Your initial response to gunfire depends mostly on your proximity to the shooter and whether or not there is cover in between. If you are within a two-second closing distance of the attacker with no cover available, leverage is established by closing the distance and going hands-on with the attacker (remember that concept of violence of action?). A two-second closing distance means it would take no more than two seconds to come face-to-face. This is actually quite a bit of time and usually comes out to be about ten to fifteen yards for the average person. If you are legally able to carry a concealed weapon and choose to do so, your positioning in the same situation will be to face and square your body to the attacker in a good, sturdy firing stance. Conversely, if you are not within a two-second closing distance or have cover available, leverage by positioning yourself behind cover and concealment, regaining your bearings, and figuring out your next course of action. The same applies if you carry concealed weapons. At this point, you have only mitigated the threat. The next steps are to gain leverage to create a tactical advantage.

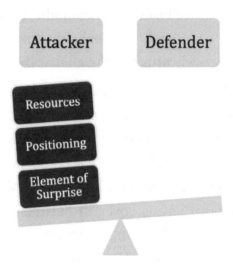

Figure 14: Tactical Advantage Before Establishing Leverage

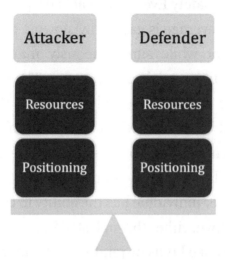

Figure 15: Tactical Advantage After Establishing Leverage

As you can see in Figures 14 and 15, once leverage is established—through physical contact or utilizing cover and concealment—the goal is to systematically gain additional leverage through positioning and employing resources. Gaining leverage switches the tempo of the attack, as the offender has lost tactical advantage and must work to regain it. If you're being attacked with a melee weapon and you are able to restrict their arm movement, you've gained an advantage where they've lost theirs. At this point, all leverage previously gained by the attacker should be negated. You may not have full control over the situation, but you are not in immediate danger of harm. In other words, the danger is still present but not as dangerous as it was before leverage was gained. It has gone from highly dangerous to just dangerous. See? Progress.

Once the Safety Event has reached a point of neutral advantage, leverage is gained by slowing the attacker's advancement while simultaneously maneuvering to gain and build a tactical advantage. The goal here is to conserve energy, using only enough to resist harm. Energy will be needed when an opportunity presents itself that enables you to either escape, de-escalate, or neutralize the threat. In combatives, this is the point where neither individual has the ability to commit to an offensive move, either through striking or a submission hold (i.e., choke holds or joint manipulation). As such, both are working to gain a position where they do have the ability to execute offensive moves. More likely than not, the attacker will be acting at a high level of energy and aggression. Maintaining good positioning while slowing the attacker's tempo will eventually lead to the attacker tiring. Once they are tired enough, you can maneuver to a position where you can either go on the offensive or restrain the attacker with complete control.

Conversely, if the offender is engaging with a firearm from outside of the two-second closing distance, utilizing cover and concealment prevents direct engagement, thereby providing an opportunity to access resources such as concealed weapons and freedom of movement. Do not always settle on the first cover and concealment position if it is not suitable for sustainment—meaning if it will not maintain a tactical advantage due to the attacker's maneuvering. Ideal cover and concealment should be big enough where you can at least move on your feet. You should have a clear field of vision, it should be made of material hard enough to stop bullet penetration, and it should provide multiple avenues for escape and maneuvering. Once you gain a tactical, advantageous position and have access to resources or reinforcement, you have reached the decisive point to end the attack by means of escape, de-escalation, or neutralization.

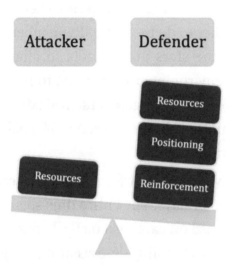

Figure 16: Tactical Advantage Before Utilizing Leverage

Figure 16 is where we want to be during a Safety Event. Utilizing leverage is the point in the engagement where you have a tactical advantage, whether by positioning, application of resources, or the presence of reinforcement. At this point, you should be able to definitively escape, de-escalate, or neutralize the threat. This should be done with violence of action, or a high level of energy, accuracy, and control. The aim is to leave no chance for the threat of harm to reoccur. To put it simply, it's "go time." Odds are this window to act will be small, but you will feel exactly when you have gained a tactical advantage and the subsequent urge to act on it. The feeling and urge to act will be instinctive and very similar to a "gut feeling" or "being in the zone." Do not overthink yourself back into a dangerous situation. Just like how you gained leverage and a tactical advantage over the attacker, it is possible for the attacker to do the same. Remember, we are not looking for the stars and planets to align, giving us the perfect environment to then act to reach our COA goal. We are looking to gain a tactical advantage to act decisively and reach the desired COA goal before the attacker gains it back.

Safety Events can last for a matter of seconds or as long as hours or days. The entire time spent in a Safety Event is focused on gaining a tactical advantage for the sole purpose of escaping, de-escalating, or neutralizing the threat—or in specific cases, delaying and resisting until reinforcements arrive. Understanding the process of establishing leverage to counteract the attacker, building on leverage to gain a tactical advantage, and taking decisive action once enough leverage is established conceptually simplifies the overall tempo of a Safety Event. Acting is not enough; you need to know when to act aggressively, when to have tactical patience, and when to act decisively. Do that, and you'll be able to turn any situation to your advantage.

Chapter 22 Review

Points of Emphasis:

❖ Tactical advantage is the state of having a greater ability to affect an opponent in relation to the effect they have on you, through means of positioning, available resources, or reinforcement.

❖ The four rules of gaining tactical advantage are: 1) Force them to "play your game." 2) Establish leverage through positioning. 3) Build leverage through positioning and resources. 4) Utilize leverage decisively through means of position, resources, and reinforcements.

Perspective:

❖ The saying goes, "It's a marathon, not a sprint." In the case of a Safety Event, however, it is a marathon, sprint, walk, and hike, all in one. If you only run at full speed, you will exhaust yourself and become vulnerable. If you only pace yourself, you will miss opportunities to establish a tactical advantage. Just like in a race, you need to calibrate your speed based on your opponents, as you only need to be one second ahead of second place to win.

Call to Action:

☐ If you take part in combatives training or scenario-based training, apply the four rules during your training sessions.

☐ Review videos of real world Safety Events, self-defense training videos, or MMA fights on YouTube (Stick with YouTube, or other trusted media sites, as searching for videos within this subject matter on the world wide web might take you to malicious sites and/or graphic videos).

☐ Take note of the attacker's actions and tempo, the victim's actions and tempo, and how leverage was utilized to affect the outcome.

Chapter 23:
Problem-Solving Mindsets

"Nothing in all Nature is more certain than the fact that no single thing or event can stand alone. It is attached to all that has gone before it, and it will remain attached to all that will follow it. It was born of some cause, and so it must be followed by some effect in an endless chain."

Julian P. Johnson

Throughout this book, we have referred back to the problem-solving cycle and how it relates to a Safety Event. The cycle, and its elements, are the more structured steps that can be followed to reach a solution. Now, we will review two mindsets that are generally used when confronting a problem. Similar to the seemingly contradictory relationship between the phrases "failure to plan is planning to fail" and "everyone has a plan until the bullets start flying," there are two mindsets that maintain the same relationship in regard to problem-solving: "one problem at a time" and "second-and third-order effects." Each has its time and place.

Each has benefits and drawbacks. The key is to know the principles of each and what scenarios they are most appropriate for.

"One problem at a time" is the idea that the only thing that is relevant at a particular time and place is the problem glaring you in the face. Once that problem has been dealt with, it is okay to begin to contemplate and solve the next problem, but not before. This is a great concept when you are dealing with a dynamic situation that seems overwhelming. Especially if you are a person who gets stressed out easily, the world can seem overwhelming when trying to solve all your problems at once. In the medical world, trauma medicine protocols are a great example of one problem at a time. In traumatic medical events, such as working as an emergency medical technician (EMT) arriving at the scene after a mass shooting, there can be many variables that need to be considered and addressed in a very quick amount of time. Oh, and people might be screaming in agony, and blood and other grotesque imagery might be present. These scenes can be overwhelming for anyone. Thankfully, trauma protocols provide a sequence of tasks that should be followed in order, which are designed to help mitigate confusion and ensure the best care provided to the injured individual(s). Here, the protocols order the "problems" from most life-threatening to least life-threatening, allowing the EMTs to focus more easily on saving lives. The same applies to Safety Events.

In a Safety Event or self-defense event, this concept is beneficial when the problem is truly and immediately life-threatening. A prime example of when "one problem at a time" is the preferred decision-making strategy is when there is a one hundred percent certainty of death if immediate action is not taken. In any scenario, an option that reduces the chance of death, even if only by 1 percent, is better than the option that gives one hundred percent chance of death. An example of this would be an event where your house has completely gone up in flames and you are trapped in the upstairs bedroom with the only viable way to safety being to jump out of the second-story window. Waiting and weighing options on how to get down in one piece would risk death by smoke inhalation, so you jump out the window and chance the less likely death by falling. In this case, it's better to be alive and have a problem like a broken leg than to be dead with no problem to worry about.

The issue that arises with the "one problem at a time" approach to problem-solving is that it can lead to unnecessary self-inflicted problems in the future. Picture this: you are driving down a shoulderless, winding mountain road during a rainstorm where you can barely see ten yards in front of you. You're driving just under the posted speed limit of fifteen miles per hour, everyone is wearing their seat belts, and you have your hands at 3 and 9 o'clock on the steering wheel because, at this moment, you are Captain Safety. You take a curve and immediately notice a downed tree blocking the entire road. You deem that you won't be able to come to a complete stop in time, so you quickly jerk the wheel toward the right shoulder, causing the vehicle to drive off the edge of the mountain cliff into a steep wooded area. You did this to solve the problem at the time, and your only thought was, "Don't run into the tree, at any cost." But now, you have a new problem: "Don't hit these many other trees," followed by, "Don't drive further down the steep decline," followed by, "How are we going to recover the vehicle?" followed by, "Do we have cell service to call for help?" and so on and so forth. The initial act might have saved you from driving into one downed tree, but now the situation is much more complicated.

This is where we have to see the forest for the trees—and in this case, literally.

"Second- and third-order effects" is a decision-making process strategy where not only is the immediate solution considered, but so are the *effects* of that solution. Truthfully, you do not need to stop consideration at the third-order effect, but usually, based on time and circumstances, you will realistically only reach the second and third. This is similar to the process of contingency planning, but now we are analyzing for future results rather than contingent scenarios happening in real time. In our house fire example, the risk of certain death causes the need for immediate action. However, going back to the example of the winding mountain road—although death is always a risk in motor vehicle crashes, the likelihood of that being the case in this scenario is not one hundred percent. The "second- and third-order effects" strategy would dictate that driving off a mountain to avoid a collision with the downed tree on the road is not advantageous for the situation as a whole. In fact, one could argue it increases the likelihood of death. With the information we have, the outcome is slightly better if you remain on the road, even if that means running into the tree. Notice I said, "slightly better," as no outcome in this situation is optimal. A second-order effect would be the collision with the downed tree, a third-order effect would be injuries sustained by occupants of the vehicle, and a fourth-order effect would begin the treatment of those injuries and calling emergency services.

And yes, I know you are poking holes in these scenarios. That's good. It lets me know you are thinking for yourself and considering all relevant and potential factors. But for the focus of this chapter, these scenarios are only meant to demonstrate the types of problem-solving mindsets that can be used when facing high-stress, high-stakes problems.

Ideally, we would like to implement solutions that have positive second- and third-order effects. However, we are not fortune tellers, so the decisions are based on information we have at the time and may ultimately not work out in our favor. This is the true principle of "second- and third-order effects": making decisions based on all present and relevant information. This is a bit involved, considering the time and resources it takes to identify, process, and analyze relevant information to be able to make a rational decision. However, when not immediately faced with imminent, life-threatening harm, this is the best route to go for your present and future.

Don't get too wrapped around the axle about when to use either of the strategies. Odds are, they will be used concurrently and subconsciously. Understanding the principles of each is enough to benefit you when reacting to and navigating Safety Events. The point is to understand problem-solving mindsets from different perspectives. Like everything we've learned, it's all about knowing which tool to use at what time, so that you can make the most out of every situation.

Chapter 23 Review

Points of Emphasis:

❖ "One problem at a time" is the strategy of focusing on one problem before considering any other, whether problems are happening concurrently or there is a possibility of other problems occurring in the future. This strategy is beneficial when the threat means certain death if not managed immediately, or in certain situations that seem overwhelming.

❖ "Second- and third-order effects" is the strategy of considering resulting rippling effects once a solution has been implemented. This strategy is beneficial when an immediate threat does not mean certain death and there is time to analyze all relative factors to ensure the best possible outcome.

Perspective:

❖ The trauma medicine protocol example of "one problem at a time" is actually a drawn-out example of the "second- and third-order effects" type of problem-solving. Essentially, medical professionals got together, looked at the data, and created an all-encompassing solution by analyzing the subsequent effects of traumatic injuries and the treatment for them, which is now packaged into a nice and neat problem-solving template. This is a perfect example of solution refinement through the continuous use of the problem-solving cycle.

Call to Action:

☐ Think of past events in your life where "one problem at a time" would have been a beneficial strategy to use. What elements would have caused the event to be a good fit for the strategy?

- ☐ Think of past events where "second- and third-order effects" would have been a beneficial strategy to use. What elements would have caused the event to be a good fit for the strategy?
- ☐ Think of past events where both strategies could have been applied. How could/can the two strategies complement each other?

End-of-Section Review

In this section, we reviewed concepts and principles that can be followed during a Safety Event. Due to the dynamic nature with varying factors during a Safety Event, this book is not able to provide specific, detailed strategies on how to counteract certain event types. Furthermore, the truth of the matter is that not every strategy works for everyone, and not every strategy will work the same way twice. However, the principles introduced in this section provide general guidance that can be universally utilized to assist you in most (if not all) situations. Understanding and mitigating your fight, flight, or freeze response enables you to act more deliberately and effectively. Being able to identify the type of incident occurring enables you to implement the appropriate SOPs and COAs. Referring to the Four Principles of Survival ensures you are thinking through important aspects that will increase the chances of survivability. Developing awareness enables you to see warning signs sooner, thereby providing you a chance to act before you are in direct danger. Understanding tactical advantage provides insight on tempo, focused efforts, and knowing when to act decisively. Lastly, understanding different conceptual mindsets and problem-solving strategies when addressing high-risk situations ensures the implementation of the thought processes behind decision-making, as all action should be deliberate.

Section Five:
The Aftermath

"The easiest period in a crisis situation is actually the battle itself. The most difficult is the period of indecision—whether to fight or run away. And the most dangerous period is the aftermath. It is then, with all his resources spent and his guard down, that an individual must watch out for dulled reactions and faulty judgment."

Richard M. Nixon

This section is intended to provide clarity, understanding, and humility to a topic that is often neglected when speaking on self-defense. The aftermath of an event is not just the immediate moments once an event has been resolved; it is *all time* after the event has occurred. This section is geared more toward the understanding of trauma while learning how to cope and heal from past events. This does not necessarily mean that individuals affected are always injured with severe emotional, physical, or spiritual trauma, as many events are resolved successfully without significant trauma or injury. However, for those who are not as fortunate, the next few chapters will provide some insight on the topics of trauma and grief, which will hopefully make the road to recovery a bit less rocky and winding.

Chapter 24:
Understanding Trauma

"Even in times of trauma, we try to maintain a sense of normality until we no longer can. That, my friends, is called surviving. Not healing. We never become whole again...we are survivors. If you are here today...you are a survivor. But those of us who have made it through hell and are still standing? We bear a different name: warriors."

Lori Goodwin

Trauma is the negative physical, emotional, and spiritual effect on a person due to a stressful event, situation, or circumstance. It can resonate and send shockwaves throughout the lives of those who were affected. Although the focus of this book is preparedness and actions during an event, the preparedness and actions post-event are just as important. This is the time when your mind tries to make sense of the why and how and everything in between. It can go on for days, weeks, months, and even years. It is during this time that we truly find ourselves. Where we find strength in hopelessness. Where we prioritize what is truly important. When we decide that there is no force stronger than ourselves.

The key to understanding trauma is the understanding that it affects everyone differently. Although there are trends and similarities, the fact is, an individual's progression of recovering from trauma can vary in time, severity, signs, and symptoms. Post-traumatic stress disorder (PTSD) is one's severe emotional and physiological response to a past event. Often, events that cause PTSD are violent in nature, but they can also be caused by sexual or verbal abuse, as well as events that cause severe emotional responses, such as death or injury of loved ones. PTSD is one of the most common manifestations of responses to trauma, so we'll be focusing on that specifically in this chapter.

PTSD manifests in the form of triggers. After witnessing or experiencing an extremely stressful event, those with PTSD may experience the effect of the event after it's happened. This can come in the form of flashbacks, nightmares, severe anxiety, and uncontrollable thoughts.

Most medical organizations categorize PTSD into four distinct symptom groups, all of which can manifest in someone suffering from PTSD. The four groups are: re-experiencing, avoidance, arousal and reactivity, and cognition and mood symptoms. Below are the four symptom groups with their respective symptoms according to the National Institute of Mental Health (NIMH):[20]

1. Re-experiencing symptoms include:
   - Flashbacks—reliving the trauma over and over, including physical symptoms like a racing heart or sweating
   - Bad dreams
   - Frightening thoughts
2. Avoidance symptoms include:
   - Staying away from places, events, or objects that are reminders of the traumatic experience
   - Avoiding thoughts or feelings related to the traumatic event
3. Arousal and reactivity symptoms include:
   - Being easily startled
   - Feeling tense or "on edge"
   - Having difficulty sleeping
   - Having angry outbursts
4. Cognition and mood symptoms include:
   - Trouble remembering key features of the traumatic event
   - Negative thoughts about oneself or the world

---

20 "Post-Traumatic Stress Disorder," National Institute of Mental Health, U.S. Department of Health and Human Services, Accessed September 16, 2022, https://www.nimh.nih.gov/health/topics/post-traumatic-stress-disorder-ptsd.

- Distorted feelings like guilt or blame
- Loss of interest in enjoyable activities

Children also may experience PTSD. However, their symptoms can be slightly different from adults. Below are some signs and symptoms of children with PTSD, according to NIMH:[21]

- Wetting the bed after having learned to use the toilet
- Forgetting how to or being unable to talk
- Acting out the scary event during playtime
- Being unusually clingy with a parent or other adult

Treatment of PTSD looks different for everyone. It may be beneficial to speak to family and friends or others who have gone through similar experiences, as there is relief in speaking through and sharing thoughts and feelings within your trusted circles. You could also speak to medical professionals who will provide options for treatment based on your signs and symptoms. No matter the type of rehabilitation you seek, remember, you are strong enough, and most importantly, you deserve peace and healing.

---

21 National Institute of Mental Health, "Post-Traumatic Stress Disorder."

Chapter 24 Review

Points of Emphasis:

- ❖ Post-traumatic stress disorder (PTSD) is a severe emotional and physiological response to a past event.
- ❖ The four symptom groups of PTSD are: re-experiencing, avoidance, arousal and reactivity, and cognition and mood symptoms.
- ❖ Treatment and rehabilitation for PTSD can come in the form of speaking with family and friends, support groups, therapy, or medication.

Perspective:

- ❖ We all go through traumatic experiences of some kind. If you're like me, you have experiences from your childhood—which you still remember clearly—that were traumatic at the time but are not so much now. I think this is due to our change in perspective and broader knowledge of the situation. Now that's not to say we were overreacting at the time or that the event itself wasn't malicious. It's only to point out that traumatic events and their lasting effects can lose their power over us as time passes and we gain perspective.

Call to Action:

☐ Talk to loved ones if you are dealing with recurring symptoms from a traumatic experience.

☐ If needed, research and visit local support groups or a medical professional in your area that specialize in trauma therapy and/or treatment.

Chapter 25:
Grief and Guilt

"Grief is not a condition to be cured but a natural part of life. Spirit does not know loss; it knows that every story begins and every story ends, yet love is eternal."

Louise L. Hay and David Kessler

Beyond understanding and coping with the traumatic event itself is the possibility of losing a loved one. In those unfortunate events where a loved one is severely injured or loses their life, the survivors are left with feelings of guilt and grief. A phenomenon most commonly referred to as "survivor's guilt" is the internal belief that the survivor has done something wrong or is somehow to blame for surviving an event when others did not. We'll be using the Five Stages of Grief, a theory developed by psychiatrist Elisabeth Kübler-Ross, to understand this emotional state. The theory explains how we endure five emotional stages after the loss of a loved one. These stages are denial, anger, bargaining, depression, and acceptance.[22] Each element gives us a better understanding of the processes we endure after losing loved ones.

Just as I graduated the Special Forces Qualification Course in 2014 and was awaiting assignment for my next duty station, my father passed away unexpectedly on Christmas Eve morning. Fortunately, I was able to spend his last days with him in the hospital. The combination of losing my father at the age of twenty-six, then immediately moving away from my family and friends and starting a brand-new chapter in my career was chaotic. Not in a physical sense, and not that anyone would have noticed, but underneath the surface, I was in turmoil, trying to make sense of it all. The entire situation would forever change the way I thought, the way I acted, and my entire outlook on life. Losing a loved one will do that.

Hopefully, you have not experienced the loss of a loved one, especially by unforeseen circumstances. But if you have, you are not alone. Now, my dad was not taken from me by acts of violence, and I know that if that was the case, my situation would be much more complicated than just dealing with the loss itself. I'm sure feelings of immense anger, and possibly hatred, would have been involved as well. That said, I wish to share my experience and outlook on loss with those

22 Editors of Psycom, "Five Stages of Grief: An Examination of the Kubler-Ross Model," Accessed April 25, 2023, https://www.psycom.net/stages-of-grief.

who have not yet experienced it, and for those who have, I hope that you may find comfort in knowing you are not alone.

Naturally, I was not immune to survivor's guilt. Survivor's guilt, as mentioned earlier, generally means one blames oneself for somehow "contributing" to the events that caused the loss or not doing enough to prevent it, even when there truly wasn't anything the person did or did not do that affected the situation. When my dad died, I immediately started questioning whether or not I could have done more to save his life and wondering whether a decision I made contributed to his death. Almost a decade later, I am no closer to having answers to those questions, and I never will. The answer I received instead is that sometimes bad things happen. That answer isn't comforting, nor is it truly productive, but it provides real perspective. Although we have the ability for extraordinary feats, we are not omnipotent nor all-knowing. As such, we cannot blame ourselves for situations of such circumstances.

The Five Stages of Grief is not a hard-and-fast rule, as we all deal with grief in our own way. It does, however, provide a general understanding of the emotions we may feel when experiencing loss. The order can vary from individual to individual, as well as the number of times a particular stage is experienced. I cannot remember the exact order or time frame of the emotions I experienced after my dad passed, but

I do remember (all too well) the feeling of denial, and how it was even present subconsciously. I would have recurring dreams that my dad was still alive. In each and every dream, all I could ever do was hug him and cry. It was only after I stopped having those dreams that I knew my mind finally accepted that my dad was indeed gone.

Denial is the mind's way of protecting us from pain. It's not exactly the act of denying that something did or did not happen, but rather a strange and eerie feeling that it's not real. Maybe it's a dream, maybe an illusion, but definitely not conceivable. Change is never easy, but loss is reality-altering. It is within this stage that your mind attempts to make sense of all that has happened, protect itself from feeling unbearable pain, and grasp the new reality that remains.

Anger shows that the mind has been able to comprehend the new reality and is now able to feel the full weight of emotion. As we begin to understand, we want the loss to make logical sense. But it doesn't. There is nothing logical about loss. Why would there be? Loss is not an opportunity or a desire. Loss provides nothing. And in this reasoning, we become angry. Angry that we could have done more, angry that others didn't do enough, angry for the fact that no matter how angry you get, it doesn't bring them back. Anger is a defense mechanism. Similar to the "fight" in a sympathetic fight, flight, or freeze response, it is meant to divert the energy outward.

Bargaining is the thinking that maybe we can somehow change the outcome or find a way to relieve the pain. During bargaining, we begin to think in "what if's." What if I did more? Maybe if I paid more attention, the event wouldn't have happened. If I was more prepared, I could have stopped it. We begin to attempt to solve a problem that is above our ability to do so. Usually, bargaining is to a higher power, or perhaps to those in positions of power. No matter who it is directed toward, bargaining is a last-ditch effort to make things right again. The issue is that the problem is no longer what we perceive it to be. The issue is within ourselves, and we must cope with a situation we can no longer influence. Rather, we must learn to accept and endure.

Depression is the understanding that no matter how angry we get, no matter how much bargaining we do, no matter what steps we try to take to reverse an outcome, the outcome remains the same. By the time we reach depression, we have fully realized the reality in which we now live. It is a cold, lonesome reality in which we seem to be powerless. And with that realization, we isolate ourselves, stop eating, and stop sleeping. We stay in bed, replaying memories over and over. In a way, there is comfort in sadness. Sadness keeps the attachment, keeps the memory, keeps the last remnants of what was. But there is a time when that must be released. This stage is unique in the fact that we are depressed because of the loss, so we indulge the sadness because it keeps the attachment—and yet, when we find ourselves recovering, we often become saddened *because* we are recovering. However, we must not measure ourselves, or our relationships, based on our emotions in one moment. Emotion is a state, not our essence. We maintain the attachment, no matter what state of emotion we are in. The goal is to foster memories within healthy and positive emotions. This is when we accept our new reality while maintaining the connection we had with our loved one.

The last stage of grief is the state of understanding, acceptance, and growth. We understand what has happened, what it has done to us and those around us, and how it will shape our future. We accept the pain, the change, and the adaptation we have had to make. And from here, we continue to grow. Grow to fill the hole that was left. Grow to take back control of our lives. Grow into the person that honors past loved ones. We remember the past, but we also look to the future.

We all experience grief, and many of us experience survivor's guilt at some point in our lives. As the saying goes, the only thing certain in life is death. Grief is a natural response to loss, but it doesn't need to consume you. Neither does survivor's guilt. No matter the situation, the reality is that life goes on, and you are allowed to move with it. It doesn't mean you forget or resist the past when it resurfaces. It just means you find the balance between past, future, and present, so you can live your life and be happy.

Chapter 25 Review

Points of Emphasis:

❖ Survivor's guilt is the internal belief that the survivor has done something wrong or is somehow to blame for surviving an event when others did not.

❖ The Five Stages of Grief is a theory developed to explain five common emotional reactions to a loss: denial, anger, bargaining, depression, and acceptance.

Perspective:

❖ Remember the Serenity Prayer: "God, grant me the serenity to accept the things I cannot change, courage to change the things I can, and wisdom to know the difference."

Call to Action:

☐ Talk to loved ones if you are dealing with recurring symptoms of grief.

☐ If needed, research and visit local support groups or a medical professional in your area that specialize in grief counseling.

Chapter 26:
Resiliency

"If you can't fly then run, if you can't run then walk, if you can't walk then crawl, but whatever you do you have to keep moving forward."

Martin Luther King Jr.

I'd like to add a sixth stage to the Five Stages of Grief. Although the Five Stages of Grief does a good job explaining one's internal turmoil and subsequent understanding, it only focuses on how loss affects us rather than how we can affect ourselves. As with all things in this book, learning to cope with grief is a continuous process and doesn't stop at acceptance, nor should it. There are times of relapse when the memory brings back anger, depression, and a lot of what if's. It is in the sixth step that we practice *resiliency*. Resiliency is the maintenance of our emotional state from past trauma, the refocus to the present space, and the unceasing pursuit of happiness, purpose, and life goals.

There were three main lessons I learned when my father passed:

1. The worst possible scenarios can happen, and when they do, they happen at a moment's notice.
2. I should have learned more from my dad when I had the chance.
3. Family is everything.

These three lessons have guided me throughout my career and life and eventually led me here, writing this book. That's not to say my life path was always clear, or that I haven't felt lost along the way. Only that since the time that my dad passed, I have used those three lessons to refocus and move me in the right direction. Within that time, I have gained an understanding of his death—but at the same time, I understand I still have a ways to go.

Realistically, I will never be the same as I was before his death—neither is anyone else when they experience loss. And why would we be? Death is life-altering. Nevertheless, I have learned patience, understanding, and—most notably—resiliency.

Defined by Merriam-Webster Dictionary, resiliency is "an ability to recover from or adjust easily to misfortune or change."[23] I would politely disagree with this definition as the phrase "recover from or adjust easily" is definitive, subjective, and unlikely. My

23 "Resilience Definition & Meaning," Merriam-Webster, Accessed March 20, 2023, https://www.merriam-webster.com/dictionary/resilience.

definition of resiliency is the ability to persist through adversity. Now, this is in general terms and could relate to any adversity, but as long as you stay in motion despite hardship or obstacles, you are resilient. Specific to the loss of a loved one, resiliency is the ability to refocus yourself back to the state of acceptance so you can maintain a sense of normalcy moving forward.

I personally allow myself to feel emotional pain when it arises. Not that I'm a sadist or enjoy pain—rather, I know that if I shield myself from it, it will just manifest itself in other ways later, more likely than not in a way that is not positive nor constructive. My intention is to feel all the emotions past trauma brings me. I don't dwell on it, but I also don't fight it. What I mean is, just like with any good moment in time, I stop to take it all in. Eventually, when the moment has passed, I continue on. The same goes with the resurgence of past trauma, like the passing of my father. When I miss him and feel pain, I allow myself to embrace and understand the pain, rather than shove it aside. However, I do not attempt to intensify it or make it more than what it is, which is just a moment. The resurgence of an emotional response shows that I have not completely processed and accepted the trauma. To ignore it would be to ignore my own growth, as it is quite difficult to grow and mature unless rooted in reality. Only then can I refocus on the present.

Refocusing on the present is the conscious effort of sensing the world around us while understanding our place in it at that moment in time. It can cause a moment of inspiration, calmness, or humbleness. Once again, this can be seen as meditation, but it doesn't need to be involved. It can be as simple as taking three deep breaths; noticing what you see, hear, smell, and feel around you; and remembering your place in this world. Our thoughts may consume us from time to time. It is our job to pull ourselves away from them when they are no longer needed in the present time. The present is constantly fleeting, and each moment is an opportunity. So, it is only to our detriment if we don't seize each opportunity in the present.

Although seen as its own step, the pursuit of long-term goals is essentially a continuation of refocusing to the present. The term "long-term goal" can be synonymous with "purpose," as the focus here is to remain steadfast in your personal journey of fulfillment. As I alluded to in the previous paragraph, we are only able to act in the present. Thereby, the pursuit of long-term goals is done by acting in the present. I know—bear with me. The point of highlighting this is so you grasp the concept that at any point in time (specifically the present) you can be working toward your goals. No matter how small the movement, progress is progress. What can sometimes seem like setbacks—like the resurgence of emotions from past trauma—is progress. In the case of emotional resurgence, it is forcing you to confront the issue. Just like any problem that you are faced with in life when it arises, it is an opportunity for improving your current situation, and more importantly, your life.

So, to help clean up this concept a bit: the present is the opportunity for growth and a means to move closer to your goals. The only way to seize the opportunity the present offers you is to maintain focus on the present, not the past. You cannot expect to get to where you want to go when always looking behind. You must look forward. And lastly, past memories are like vacation spots. They are nice to visit, but we really shouldn't live there. Use them when they are beneficial, and continue on once they have served their purpose. Eventually, they'll leave you a stronger, more resilient person.

Chapter 26 Review

Points of Emphasis:

❖ In general, resiliency is the ability to persist through adversity. When dealing with the loss of a loved one, resiliency is the ability to refocus yourself back to the state of acceptance so you can maintain a sense of normalcy.

❖ Refocus yourself to the present when dwelling on the past by mindful breathing, sensing the world around you through your five senses, and focusing on your importance in the world at that moment in time.

❖ Focus on your Life Goals and aspirations when feeling lost. Life Goals serve as your motivation and guide to ensure you focus on what is important in your life.

Perspective:

❖ Memories can bring us joy, pain, inspiration, regret, pride, guilt, and everything in between. It is easy for us to allow the memory to influence our emotions as if it is happening in real time all over again. However, it is important to understand that it is, in fact, not happening. Similar to when we leave the movie theater after an emotionally compelling movie, we must realize that the world has been moving along without us as we transition back to the "real world." It's okay to visit the "movie theater", but living there is unsustainable.

Call to Action:

☐ If not done already, write down your Life Goals and place them in a location where you will see them daily. This will act as your daily reminder of your purpose and your place in the world.

Chapter 27:
After-Action Review

"We do not learn from experience...we learn from reflecting on experience."

John Dewey

L ife is full of learning through experience, mistakes, and trial and error. We must maintain a process to reflect on those experiences by building on the good and learning from the not-so-good. The military has a practice of reviewing past actions to ensure things that work remain a part of the plan and things that do not work are modified or thrown out completely. These processes are called After-Action Reviews, or AARs for short. Previously mentioned in Chapter 17, we will discuss them in detail here.

I chose to put this chapter after the chapters focusing on grief to emphasize the importance of emotional health before revisiting the event in a constructive capacity. Although AARs are primarily used immediately after the completion of a mission,

I don't believe they are productive when individuals are still processing emotional trauma. In the cases where an individual or individuals may be dealing with PTSD, AARs should be postponed until there is at least an understanding of how it is affecting those involved. Even then, it might be good practice to omit the portions that trigger PTSD episodes or allow those individuals to excuse themselves if need be.

With that being said, AARs are not something the military invented or exclusively use, but I do believe the way they are conducted creates an environment of understanding and development. AARs begin with the full narrative of the event told from each person's perspective, followed by each person providing at least two points of sustainment and two points for improvement. "Sustainment" is the term used for actions taken or methods that should continue. "Improvement" is the term used for actions taken or methods that should be modified or discarded completely.

AARs should be seen as a general meeting with the purpose being to educate everyone on the entire narrative, based on all perspectives, with the goal of formulating best practices. The meeting should be managed by one individual—I recommend the head of the household or whoever is in charge of creating the Safety Plans to be in charge of running the AARs. Normally, the narrative is started from the beginning by the individual who had first contact with the threat or first initiated a Safety Plan. From there, the narrative can bounce from individual to individual based on the flow of the narrative. It is important to not jump too far ahead in the narrative when there are different perspectives that can speak on a particular part. So, be sure to segment the narrative by major movement pieces. For example, a breakdown of major movements after enacting a Home Invasion Safety Plan would be the initial contact up to calling 911, the 911 call up to meeting up in the master bedroom, and maintaining security in the master bedroom up to when the police arrived. By breaking up the narrative into clearly defined segments, it will be easier to follow along while putting all the pieces together and ensuring all aspects of the event are reviewed. Talking through sustainments and improvements is done once the narrative is reviewed completely through each participant's perspective.

During the last portion of the AAR, each individual is able to provide two sustainments and two improvements. It can really be any number, but I recommend two since this will provide a bit of quantity and content to go off of when formulating best practices. This should be as specific as possible, since comments like, "I think we did a good job calling 911," or "I think our meet-up spot was not good," do not provide a foundation to build upon. Rather, the comments should be along the lines of, "I think it was a good call planning for the person closest to the master bedroom to immediately call 911," or "I think the meet-up spot was a bad spot because it wasn't clearly marked and could not be seen from my vantage point." Obviously, the more details the better, but remember that it will ultimately be the consensus of the group or heads of the household that will make the call on whether to modify the existing Safety Plan. It is also good practice to write down the sustainments and improvements, as they can be continuously referred to during the time a Safety Plan is being modified or revisited.

Once the AAR is completed, everyone should be able to clearly state what other individuals did during the event and what worked and did not work. This is something that might feel awkward the first time around, but with practice, it becomes a useful tool that can also be implemented in other facets of our lives, such as business, sports, or general daily logistics.

Chapter 27 Review

Points of Emphasis:

❖ After-Action Reviews (AARs) are structured conversations conducted after a particular event that reviews what went right, what went wrong, and how to improve the process for future implementation.

❖ Besides the full narrative and all perspectives thereof, the AAR should identify sustainments (elements that should continue to be part of the plan) and improvements (elements that should be discarded or changed).

❖ AARs are objective and constructive, and they are not meant to point fingers or cast blame. It is a developmental process to ensure best practices are being used in a particular situation.

Perspective:

❖ Athletes review past game films to, essentially, conduct AARs. As we do not have the ability to always record ourselves and review the film, we must instead rely on our memory and the perspective of others to recreate and critique the events that transpired. This is why it is important to conduct AARs as soon as possible and to speak truthfully, as any misconception of the event will cause unneeded deviation.

Call to Action:

☐ Review the After-Action Review (AAR) Checklist in the CTA Workbook.

☐ Conduct an AAR after group training sessions, rehearsals, and after Safety Events.

End-of-Section Review

In this section, we reviewed the possible effects and aftermath of Safety Events. In any event, there is a chance of lingering trauma, injury, and death. Just as we prepare ourselves for these types of dangerous situations, we must take care of ourselves and others after the fact. Understanding trauma, survivor's guilt, and the elements of grief provide you with intrapersonal insight and the ability to implement appropriate rehabilitation. Practicing resilience enables you to push through times of hardship while maintaining physical, mental, emotional, and spiritual well-being. Lastly, by implementing AARs, you will be able to foster continuous positive progression and development.

Conclusion

Even if you live in one of the safest parts of the country and never felt as though you were in danger of harm, self-defense is a range of skills you need—though we all wish we would never have to use them. We pay hundreds and sometimes thousands of dollars each year to insurance companies just in case bad things happen to our home, automobile, health, and life. Unlike insurance, self-defense pays us back in dividends. If you have experience investing, you know your money should be working for you. When you invest in yourself, specifically through development and training, you not only decrease the risk of something bad happening, but you also increase the chances of good things happening. As stated in the introduction, this book's focus is on security and protection concepts that promote prevention, safety, and personal empowerment. Indirectly, most principles in this book (and the skills learned in self-defense practices) can be applied to any and all aspects of one's life. These are called transferable skills, which have unlimited application.

Yes, I want you to be safe, protected, and free from fear that you or your loved ones are at risk from harm. But just as importantly—if not more so—I want you to live your *best* life, because it gives you purpose, fulfillment, and joy. If you do happen to live in fear of or with constant threat from harm, your next best step is to protect and enable yourself, with the assistance of this book and other resources. If you feel as though you are relatively safe but there is always that chance of vulnerability, you should integrate the principles with your typical habits to reinforce your safety. If you are not convinced that self-defense consideration is necessarily needed because our society has measures in place to prevent harm, I would ask for you to broaden your perspective and take notice of the atrocities that happen on a daily basis.

Danger will always be present. Bad people will always exist. But we are not victims. We are not at the mercy of others. We are forces to be reckoned with. We are people with purpose. We are people of action.

We only get one life. So make it your best.

Complementary Readings

Below are the top ten books I recommend that will provide additional or complementary information related to the subject matters of this book. All together, these resources will help you achieve a well-rounded strategy to boost confidence and performance while supporting your Safety and Life Goals.

❖ *Man's Search for Meaning* - By Viktor E. Frankl
❖ *Your Best Year Ever: A 5-Step Plan for Achieving Your Most Important Goals* - By Michael Hyatt
❖ *Peak Performance: Elevate Your Game, Avoid Burnout, and Thrive with the New Science of Success* - By Brad Stulberg and Steve Magness
❖ *10-Minute Toughness: The Mental Training Program for Winning Before the Game Begins* - By Jason Selk
❖ *Atomic Habits: An Easy & Proven Way to Build Good Habits & Break Bad Ones* - By James Clear
❖ *The Law of Self Defense: The Indispensable Guide to the Armed Citizen* - By Andrew F. Branca
❖ *The Gift of Fear* - By Gavin de Becker

- ❖ *Never Split the Difference: Negotiating As If Your Life Depended On It* - By Chris Voss with Tahl Raz
- ❖ *How to Win Friends and Influence People* - By Dale Carnegie
- ❖ *Whoever Fights Monsters: My Twenty Years Tracking Serial Killers for the FBI* - By Robert K. Ressler and Tom Shachtman

Bibliography

"Law Enforcement." Bureau of Justice Statistics. Accessed February 16, 2023. https://bjs.ojp. gov/topics/law-enforcement.

"obsession." In *New Oxford American Dictionary*, edited by Stevenson, Angus, and Christine A. Lindberg. : Oxford University Press, 2010. https:// www-oxfordreference-com.ezproxy.umgc .edu/view/10.1093/acref/9780195392883 .001.0001/m_en_us1272710.

"preparedness." In *New Oxford American Dictionary*, edited by Stevenson, Angus, and Christine A. Lindberg. : Oxford University Press, 2010. https://www-oxfordreference-com.ezproxy. umgc.edu/view/10.1093/acref/978019 5392883.001.0001/m_en_us1280408.

"Resilience Definition & Meaning." Merriam-Webster. Accessed March 20, 2023. https://www.merri-am-webster.com/dictionary/resilience.

"Transgressor Definition & Meaning." Dictionary. com. Accessed March 15, 2022. https://www. dictionary.com/browse/transgressor.

Addiction Resource Editorial Staff. "Behavioral Addictions: Causes, Signs, and Treatment Options." Addiction Resource, August 10, 2021. https://www.addictionresource.net/ behavioral-addictions/.

District of Columbia v. Heller, 554 U.S. 570 (2008).

Editors of Psycom. "Five Stages of Grief: An Examination of the Kubler-Ross Model." Accessed April 25, 2023. https://www.psycom.net/stages-of-grief.

Engrossed Bill of Rights, September 25, 1789; General Records of the United States Government; Record Group 11; National Archives.

Frankl, Viktor E., Harold S. Kushner, and William J. Winslade. Man's search for meaning. Boston, MA: Beacon Press, 2006.

Grant, Jon E, Liana RN Schreiber, and Brian L Odlaug. "Phenomenology and Treatment of Behavioural Addictions." *The Canadian Journal of Psychiatry* 58, no. 5 (2013): 252–59. https:// doi.org/10.1177/070674371305800502.

Kaufman, Stephen F. *Art of War : The Definitive Interpretation of Sun Tzu's Classic Book of Strategy.* New York: Tuttle Publishing, 2012. https://search-ebscohost-com.ezproxy.

umgc.edu/login.aspx?direct=true&db=nleb-k&AN=1567300&site=eds-live&scope=site.

Mackworth, N. H. "The Breakdown of Vigilance during Prolonged Visual Search." *Quarterly Journal of Experimental Psychology* 1, no. 1 (1948): 6–21. https://doi.org/10.1080/17470214808416738 https://doi.org/10.1080/17470214808416738

Mayo Clinic Staff. "Obsessive-Compulsive Disorder (OCD)." Mayo Clinic. Mayo Foundation for Medical Education and Research, March 11, 2020. https://www.mayoclinic.org/diseases-conditions/obsessive-compulsive-disorder/symptoms-causes/syc-20354432.

Mayo Clinic. "Antisocial Personality Disorder." February 24, 2023. https://www.mayoclinic.org/diseases-conditions/antisocial-personality-disorder/symptoms-causes/syc-20353928.

McDonald v. City of Chicago, 561 U.S. 742 (2010).

Mulder, Th. "Motor Imagery and Action Observation: Cognitive Tools for Rehabilitation." *Journal of Neural Transmission* 114, no. 10 (2007): 1265–78. https://doi.org/10.1007/s00702-007-0763-z.

N.Y. State Pistol & Rifle Association v. Bruen, 142 S. Ct. 2111 (2022).

National Institute of Mental Health. "Post-Traumatic Stress Disorder." U.S. Department of Health and Human Services. Accessed September 16, 2022. https://www.nimh.nih.gov/health/topics/post-traumatic-stress-disorder-ptsd.

People v. La Voie, 155 Colo. 551, 395 P.2d 1001 (1964).

The American Institute of Stress. "What Is Stress?" January 4, 2017. https://www.stress.org/what-is-stress.

Help Others!

Thank You For Reading My Book!

Please share if this book has brought you peace of mind, confidence, and most of all, the tools needed to keep you and your loved ones safe.

.

Others may not know about this book or may be hesitant to make the purchase. Your input may prove to be the deciding factor in them taking action.

Please take two minutes now to leave a helpful review on Amazon letting potential readers know what you thought of the book:

Thank you for your support!

- John

Made in United States
Troutdale, OR
11/03/2023

14199101R00186